Harmony
From the
Inside Out

Harmony
From the
Inside Out

Creating and Living Your
Performance Potential

by
Jan Carley

Copyright © 2009 by Jan Carley

All rights reserved. This book, or parts thereof, may not be reproduced in any form without written permission of the author except for the inclusion of brief quotations in a review.

Many names and identifying details of the client stories in this book have been changed to preserve confidentiality.

Published by:
Creative Coaching Group Publishing
775 Sawyer's Lane
Vancouver, B.C. V5Z 3Z8
CANADA

Printed in Canada
ISBN: 978-0-9812377-0-1

First printing 2009

Library and Archives Canada Cataloguing in Publication

Carley, Jan
     Harmony from the inside out: creating and living your performance potential / by Jan Carley.

Includes bibliographical references.

ISBN 978-0-9812377-0-1

     1. Self-actualization (Psychology). 2. Achievement motivation.
3. Performing arts – Psychological aspects. I. Title.

BF637.S4C378 2009   158.1   C2009-904862-0

Author Contact:
Jan Carley
jan@creativecoachinggroup.com
www.creativecoachinggroup.com

Cover Design: me&lewis ideas inc., Vancouver, B.C. www.meehanlewis.com
Book Design and Layout: Deb Carfrae, DLC Designs, www.dlcdesigns.net

This book is dedicated with love and gratitude to
Sandy Marron
and the women of Lions Gate Chorus
for their inspiration and support

CONTENTS

Harmony From the Inside Out

Creating and Living Your Performance Potential

INTRODUCTION

Back in high school, I went on a date with a boy to a concert in which his dad was singing in a barbershop quartet. I wasn't expecting much from the men in striped jackets and straw boater hats, but I liked the boy, so I went. I was happily shocked by the visceral reaction I had listening to his dad's quartet sing a stunningly moving rendition of *Oh Danny Boy*. I quite unexpectedly felt the hairs raise on my arms and tears well in my eyes. That was my first exposure to the power of harmony.

Many years later I heard about the Sweet Adelines, the women's organization singing a cappella four-part harmony in the barbershop style. Remembering how moved I had been by *Oh Danny Boy*, and wanting to give myself an outlet for singing, which I loved and hadn't done much of recently, I visited a rehearsal of Lions Gate Chorus, in Vancouver, British Columbia, Canada, in November 1994.

The rest, as they say, is history. I have now been singing barbershop harmony with the Lions Gate Chorus for almost 15 years. Something about the joy of singing with a group, the weekly rush of endorphins and the incredible feeling of singing tight harmonies, creating ringing chords and screaming overtones, has hooked me.

Little did I know that my once-a-week hobby (ha!) would turn into a lifetime passion. Not only would it include incredible performance experiences, it would connect intimately with my mid-life career change to professional business and personal coaching as well as inspire me to write this book.

My professional work life had, to that point, been in theatre, in the performing arts. I saw a chance to bring my training to this hobby group of singers and began to work as Artistic Director on the Lions Gate Chorus' annual shows. Working with 100+ women from all walks of life, of all ages and professions, was a challenging and fascinating experience. I quickly found that the biggest part of creating a memorable show was to motivate, inspire and instill trust and confidence in the singers/performers so the best of who they were could shine. It became not so much about my artistic vision, the script, the staging, the lighting or the content, as about how to help create the optimal conditions for performers to connect and communicate with the audience.

At the same time, I decided I needed to get closer to helping people connect with themselves and each other, so I embarked on the amazing profession of business and personal coaching. With the guidance of my mentor, Carollyne Conlinn, I enrolled in the transformational executive coaching program at Royal Roads University in Victoria, British Columbia. I knew then that I had found my life's work.

Music is a passion for many. According to a Chorus Impact Study done by Chorus America (www.chorusamerica.org), there are an estimated 32.5 million adults regularly singing in one of over 270,000 choruses in the USA today.

It occurred to me, therefore, that if the coaching work I do could add to the joy and enjoyment of those singing in choruses and choirs, that that could be a really huge and profound contribution to make. I saw how applying the inner coaching principles could add to the happiness one feels, not only while performing, but also in the rest of one's life. I began my work as the "Inner Coach of Barbershop," coaching directors and chorus members throughout North America on the principles in this book. The response was huge, and after receiving testimonials from person after person on how this "group" coaching spilled over for positive effect in their personal and business lives, I decided to write this book.

Is this book just for singers? Absolutely not! The content of, and exercises in, this book are easily applied principles to create key shifts and fulfillment in any part of your life.

As you will discover on the pages to follow, I am a passionate believer in the power of positivity and that your life is what you create it to be. There is no magic formula – there is nothing you need to buy, assemble or otherwise put together to achieve "harmony from the inside out"… that is the most excellent thing about this work. Everything you need you already have inside. I believe all of us have the capacity to experience true joy, to live authentically and connect with our world. Sometimes we just need help to access the "how" in order to let it out, cherish it, nurture it and celebrate it.

My hope is that you will use this book in whatever way feels right for you – read it all at once, stop and do the exercises, skip around. For maximum effectiveness I recommend that you buy a journal (it can be a steno pad or a leather bound) and begin to record your thoughts as you work through the reflection questions and embark on this journey.

In closing, if this material in any way touches you, changes you, inspires you, or motivates you to begin to live life to its fullest, then I am a happy woman. I welcome hearing your comments and your ideas of what you need and want to help you achieve "harmony from the inside out." Email me at jan@creativecoachinggroup.com and I promise to respond to you.

Success is the art of being who you already are...

Harmony awaits!

1

THE "A" GAME
Living in Possibility

*"You and I are essentially infinite choice-makers.
In every moment of our existence, we are in that field of all
possibilities where we have access to an infinity of choices."*

– Deepak Chopra[1]

As we begin our quest to achieve harmony from the inside out, we must start with the very foundation of our lives – the bricks and mortar upon which we will build the rest of our world – the fundamental principle to shift our thinking into an infinite world of possibility.

The foundation of all of our work together is an approach to life called the "Appreciative Approach," or as I like to refer to it, playing the "A" Game. This is the one principle to which I hope you will really pay attention and embrace. It may be the biggest shift you make in your life and work.

The "A" Game uses principles of an organizational approach called "Appreciative Inquiry" pioneered by professors David Cooperrider and Suresh Srivastva in the 1980s. Organizational consultants around the world increasingly are embracing an appreciative approach to bring about collaborative and strengths-based change in organizations. "Appreciative Inquiry (AI) is an exciting way to embrace organizational change. Its assumption is simple: Every organization has something that works right – things that give it life when it is most alive, effective, successful and

---

1 Deepak Chopra is a world-renowned author and speaker in the field of mind-body healing. www.deepakchopra.com

AI   appreciative Inquiry —

connected in healthy ways to its stakeholders and communities. AI begins by identifying what is positive and connecting to it in ways that heighten energy and vision for change."[2]

What a concept! Imagine looking at your world – your work, your home, your chorus – in the context of identifying what *is* working and then consciously building on those strengths to create the changes you want. The "A" Game also embraces making a shift in how we look at individuals – be they colleagues, partners, offspring or fellow chorus members.

"Appreciative Inquiry deliberately seeks to discover people's exceptionality – their unique gifts, strengths, and qualities. It actively searches and recognizes people for their specialties – their essential contributions and achievements. Appreciative Inquiry builds momentum and success because it believes in people. It really is an invitation to a positive revolution."[3]

Simply put – the Appreciative Approach is an asset-based approach to life. Most of us have been taught, trained and been rewarded for using a problem-solving approach – that is, to look for what isn't working, figure out what the problem is, analyze it and then think up ways to fix the problem and put an action plan in place to do so. The problem-solving approach is a deficit-based approach that focuses on what is wrong. The "A" Game would have us identify what *is* working, and imagine and create what *could be* and then implement the action toward the new possibility.

Imagine shifting one's focus to identifying what is working now – the strengths – and thinking of the potential and how to leverage, expand and grow from that. Imagine spending your time in the world of "what is possible," instead of "what isn't possible."

This approach is important because it gives us an opportunity to move forward and opens up a world of possibility. In the highly technical world of a cappella choral singing, focusing on what is *right* may well be the hardest principle to swallow (especially for our masterfully technical directors and musical leaders). Isn't the whole idea of a technical art form to find the mistakes and fix them? What possible improvements in technical ability could be made by focusing on individual and collective strengths – on what is right rather than what needs to be improved?

---

2   Cooperrider, David L.; Whitney, Diana; and Stavros, Jacqueline M., *Appreciative Inquiry Handbook: The First in a Series of AI Workbooks for Leaders of Change*, Lakeshore Communications, 2003, pp. XVII-XIX

3   Cooperrider, D.L. et al (Eds.), *Lessons from the Field: Applying Appreciative Inquiry*, Thin Book Publishing, 2001, p. 12

Herein lies the biggest misunderstanding about playing the "A" Game – about taking an appreciative approach. The approach is a foundation, a guiding principle, and does not mean that one abandons attention to detail or commitment to excellence, nor does it eliminate working to improve technical mastery.

The Appreciative Approach actually creates a better environment for learning. When not bound by the fear and limitations of doing something wrong, one is free to explore the possibilities of doing right.

Back in August 2007, Lions Gate Chorus Master Director, Sandy Marron, was frustrated with the less than commanding vocal authority and confidence of her lead section. (In a cappella Barbershop Harmony, the "Lead" section sings the recognizable melody line and is considered to be pivotal in establishing the "personality" of the chorus.) Typical great lead personalities are characterized by mega-personality, charisma, presence and brash confidence.

With only three months left before the International a cappella chorus singing competition, Sandy was beginning to panic – without the lead section stepping up to the plate and taking command, the chorus' hopes of achieving its Top Ten goal were dim. A survey of the Lead Section in August 2007 showed that only 20% considered themselves to be "Top Ten" lead singers. Wow. This was a serious problem. How could she best achieve what she wanted?

As Sandy became more tense dealing with the enormity of this problem, she began trying to get what she wanted from the leads by sheer force. As you can imagine, quite the reverse of what Sandy wanted to happen, happened – the lead section knew they weren't doing well; they lost even more confidence and became afraid of doing something wrong. They began to sing to please the director, or, to avoid disappointing the director. Effectively, their energy became drawn inward, became self-focused and possibilities for learning and improvement were completely shut down at that point. Forward motion was stalled and the chorus' prospects looked bleak.

Sandy is a masterful and innovative director, and not afraid to take risks. Knowing that she needed to do something differently, she opened herself up to individual coaching with me to work on her approach and her "intention" for rehearsals (see Chapter 7).

She shifted to the "A" Game and incorporated regular and specific acknowledgement of the lead section into every rehearsal. Rather than badger the section about what they weren't doing well, she began regularly to reinforce what they were doing right. By changing her approach to one of appreciating the value, strength and potential of the lead section, and focusing on what they were doing right and then leveraging that to build confidence, Sandy's mastery of the appreciative approach created an open environment of learning and possibility.

I noticed an amazing shift in Sandy – and the almost immediate shift in the lead section was astonishing. A subsequent survey of the section showed that 80% now considered themselves to be "Top Ten" lead singers! Adopting the appreciative approach in no small part contributed to Lions Gate Chorus taking the 2007 International Singing Competition by storm and leaping from a 12th place ranking to a 3rd place Bronze medal placement.

The "A" Game creates a learning environment of capacity, imagination, possibility, energy and positivity. The appreciative approach acknowledges the contribution of individuals in order to increase trust, empower individuals and create organizational congruency. David L. Cooperrider[4] said that by paying special attention to "the best of the past and present" we can "ignite the collective imagination of what might be."

The "A" Game is a new way of "being" in the world that creates possibilities for the future in any area of our lives.

- The opportunities for learning and growth are expanded because we have placed ourselves in a space of unlimited possibility.
- Our thoughts are freed from the constraints of any limiting boundaries and we have options.
- Situations that seemed stuck or frozen become liberated.
- The possibilities of moving forward are magnified.

---

4 Dr. David Cooperrider, Ph.D. is best known for co-founding the organizational approach of Appreciative Inquiry (AI) which is creating a positive revolution in the leadership of change.

REFLECTION QUESTIONS

1. How could using an appreciative approach and playing the "A" Game shift possibilities and build capacity in the different areas of your life?

2. What could happen in your place of business and with your work team if you took an asset-based approach?

3. How could the "A" Game open up communication possibilities with your family or other relationships?

4. What might happen if you begin to incorporate an appreciative approach into your chorus life or other high-achieving team?

WHERE'S YOUR FOCUS?

A long time ago, long before the notion of coaches was around, I was working for a company that brought in a consultant for a workshop to get all of the managers motivated. I don't remember much from that day except for a small handout she gave us at the end of the workshop with a diagram on it entitled "Where's your focus?." On the left hand side of the sheet it said, *Don't have, don't want* and on the right side it said *Do have, do want.* I taped that piece of paper to the side of my fridge where, fifteen years later, yellowed and splattered with grease stains, it reminds me daily of one of the fundamental keys to happiness.

Where we focus our minds and energy in our lives is one thing that is completely in our control, completely our choice and has a monumental effect on our joy and well-being. Where do you place *your* focus? Unfortunately, the *don't have, don't want* side of the ledger is the default for many of us and leads nowhere. All it does is make you feel bad and there is no way out of that place until you flip over to the *do have, do want* side.

For example, let's say you are deep in debt and don't have two nickels to rub together. Okay – so you *don't have* money and you *don't want* to be in debt. If you keep your mental focus there, what can you do with that? How can you make any movement out of debt?

If you flip your focus to the other side, the possibilities instantly open up. What do you want? "I *do want* to have enough money to pay off my debt, pay my bills and have enough left over to live." Now you have somewhere to go. Now you can begin to think of concrete strategies to reduce your debt, access more resources, set some goals, and create an action plan.

While you are focusing on the *don't have, don't want* side you are paralyzed in the land of scarcity: scarcity thinking. Shifting to the *do have, do want* side opens up a world of abundance, a world of infinite possibility. A simple shift of where you place your focus can change your life.

"…but Jan," you say, "sometimes there is just mess in my life. I can't be positive all the time." Absolutely… $)%*^ happens! No, you don't have to put a positive spin on everything, and, yes, it is just crappy that, say, you got laid off from your job. What I am talking about is the one thing that you do have control over, and that is about where you choose to put your focus – even after something crappy happens. Sure, give yourself time to wallow – get mad, cry, whatever... but then you can make a choice on where are you going to continue to focus: on what you don't have (e.g., a job) or what you do want (e.g., a new job that you like even more, that pays even better.) Now *that* is something to work with.

✴ This is about focus. This has nothing to do with optimism, nothing to do with positivity. It has everything to do with possibility. It has everything to do with options. By focusing on what we want rather than what we don't want, we instantly get unstuck and free up our thinking. Remember, when we put energy to something, it magnifies. What do you want to magnify? Where is your focus? What possibilities open up if you shift to *do have, do want?*

The principles are absolutely compelling for all parts of your life and pretty much any situation. For example, let's say, the Board of Directors of your chorus is spending a lot of time at their board meeting moaning about how they can't get chorus members to volunteer for the myriad of jobs that are critical to keeping the chorus running. In their inspiring book, *The Art of Possibility*, Rosamund Stone Zander and Benjamin Zander would say that the Board has embarked on "downward spiral talk" which is a "resigned way of speaking that excludes possibility."[5]

By shifting to the other side of the "Where's Your Focus?" awareness grid and focusing on what they want, the Board can instantly shift to the world of possibility. They might say, "We want more active volunteers so that the chorus runs smoothly." Okay, now they can get into the action planning around that possibility. They might ask, "How can we make it attractive for folk to volunteer?" and "What could we do differently to approach this ongoing challenge?"

Let's take a parenting example to illustrate how focusing on what you want engages and creates conversation with a possibility of going somewhere, and focusing on what you don't want often is a conversation ender:

Scenario 1: Focusing On What You Don't Want

Parent: "Johnny, I don't want to see your socks all over your bedroom floor – your room is a mess."

Johnny: Grunts "humph" and goes on reading.

---

5 Rosamund Stone Zander and Benjamin Zander, *The Art of Possibility* (New York: Penguin Books 2002) p. 108.

Scenario 2: Focus On What You Do Want
Parent: "Johnny, I would like you to pick up your dirty socks and put them in the laundry hamper please, so that your room is clean before our house guests arrive."
Johnny: Grunts "humph"... but puts the socks away.

Notice how a shift in focus could play out at a chorus rehearsal. Let's say the baritones are consistently singing flat in a particular section of a song. If you, as a musical leader, approach this by saying to the baritones, "You are singing flat," it leaves them with nowhere to go. A simple shift to: "Baritones, I need you to lighten up your vocal quality and sing sharper in Bars 7-13," the baritones have an instruction on which they can take action. You can't take action and move forward when you are focused on what you don't have and don't want. It is impossible. By a simple shift to what you want to grow and what could be better, you create a new level of energy that moves you into action.

Meghan had had a brutal day. As a beautiful, intelligent young woman, you would think she had the world at her fingertips – but Meghan has dystonia, a neurological movement disorder she got as a result of a brain tumor and hemorrhage at age thirteen. That hasn't stopped her from becoming a nationally ranked horseback rider in dressage, or singing and doing energetic choreography as a valued member of a world-class a cappella chorus. On most days, it did not affect her positive, optimistic attitude, but today was different. Meghan had fallen victim to the economic downturn and that very day had been laid off from her mid-level marketing job.

After crying all day, she arrived at a Lions Gate Chorus rehearsal that night in a desperate state. It is hard enough getting a job in tough economic times, but when you have a physical disability that allows only partial use of the left side of your body and results in chronic muscle pains and spasms that severely limit physical movement, well – Meghan was feeling very distressed at that point and pessimistic about her future. Focused in a bad place, she hoped that a chorus singing rehearsal would take her out of her funk. I had been working with Lions Gate Chorus coaching them over several months in a holistic program to help them achieve inner and outer mastery and coincidently that night was the very night I explored the "Where's Your Focus?" concept in a workshop with the chorus members.

"It was so cool and synchronistic," Meghan explained. "I felt really crappy, and all of sudden Jan was asking us to look at our lives and see where we were focusing our energy. I suddenly was rocked out of my bad space and given the gift of perspective. I flashed back to the early days of my dystonia diagnosis, when I lay on the couch for days, depressed, as I realized that I would have to give up my dreams of playing guitar, piano and French horn because I didn't have mobility in my left arm. I reminded myself of the lesson that I learned then, that things always look worse when you are in the middle of them, and if I stepped back, and if I started focusing on what I had in my life and what I wanted, then I had options and there were possibilities. My life hadn't ended."

Meghan realized that she had a choice. She could stay focused on what she didn't have (a job) and what she didn't want (to be unemployed) or she could begin to shift and create what she did want in her life and from her next job.

Three weeks later Meghan told me: "You totally helped me get focused and grounded and gave me techniques to refocus my energies. I now realize that there is no stigma attached to being laid off in an economic slowdown and in that way I feel less of a victim. I am optimistic and know that things will pick up from here. I'm kind of loving the time off right now and am ridiculously happy." (Three months later Meghan successfully landed her "dream job" and is now working in philanthropy for a renowned children's hospital foundation.)

Where's your Focus? Like Meghan rediscovered, we can choose where we place our focus, and just as easily, we can choose to place it somewhere else.

INDIVIDUAL EXERCISE: WHERE'S YOUR FOCUS?

First it is important to be aware of where you are putting your focus and energy in the different areas of your life. You may find that for certain areas of your life you are living in possibility and abundance thinking and in other parts of your life you are woefully mired in scarcity thinking. Fill out the awareness grid on page 11 and notice where you are putting your energy. On which side of the grid are you focusing? Think about what could happen if you shifted to the "*Do have, do want*" focus... to the space of unlimited possibility. Choose an area and consciously make that shift.

WHERE'S YOUR FOCUS? Awareness Grid

	Don't Have / Don't Want	Do Have / Do Want
Relationships (family, friends, romantic)		
Health & Fitness		
Money/ Finances		
Work/ Career		
Home		
Recreation & Free time		

CHORUS EXERCISE: WHERE'S YOUR FOCUS?

The same exercise is an easy one to adapt to chorus life. Create your own grid for the musical leadership and the management teams of the chorus to fill out with the details of their respective areas of responsibility listed on the left hand side. Have the leadership teams fill out both sides of the grid (the **Don't Have, Don't Want** side and the **Do Have, Do Want** side). Have the teams notice where their focus is being put.

In the appropriate areas, make a conscious effort to collectively shift that focus and explore the possibilities of living on the **Do Have, Do Want** side. What possibilities might open up for chorus members, or for the chorus as a whole if that shift was made? Create an action plan to make that shift. Enroll the chorus members in your new, reframed approach.

2

GETTING IN TUNE
Clearing your Inner Static

"What lies behind us and what lies before us are tiny matters compared to what lies within us."

– Ralph Waldo Emerson

As I sit at my desk writing a chapter about how interference can get in the way of achieving one's performance potential, I have to smile at the irony as I think of the list of external interferences that have gotten in my way this morning alone! Let's see now – the phone rang, my email beckoned, I felt a bit peckish, I ate some praline ice cream (yum), I got an ice cream headache, the phone rang again, I had to check my email again. Those were just the external interferences. I won't even get started on the internal interferences!

Suffice it to say, unless you live solo on a deserted island due south of Chile, you are pretty constantly bombarded by distractions and interferences that easily can get in the way of you achieving what you want in your performance and life. A key element of moving into your performance potential and achieving your goals is learning how to reduce (and ideally eliminate) as many of those interferences (both external and internal) as possible.

In *The Inner Game of Music*, a brilliant book written by Barry Green and W. Timothy Gallwey about how to master the "inner game" for more joy and success in performing, the authors describe a simple equation for Performance success.

$$P = p - i$$

In their equation, the large **P** refers to your Peak Performance, which is ultimately whatever result you are capable of achieving. The small *p* stands for your potential, which refers to your ability and your "technical" skill, and *i* means interference – the external and internal things that get in the way.

"Most people try to improve their performance **(P)** by increasing their potential *(p)* through practicing and learning new skills. The Inner Game approach, on the other hand, is to reduce interference *(i)* at the same time that potential *(p)* is being trained – and the result is that our actual performance comes closer to our true potential."[6]

In my role as the Inner Coach of Barbershop, I do inner coaching work with competitive a cappella choruses throughout North America to prepare them mentally for high-level international singing competitions. I have discovered that there is one more piece that is critical to add to Green and Gallwey's performance equation. In order to really live your own personal performance potential, you must add the missing ingredient of *"a"* – Attitude. Your mind-set is a critical partner in your quest for success in any part of your life. Without a positive mental attitude, 100% focus, and belief in yourself, your technical mastery – your "potential" if you will, will never be fully realized.

So, with great respect to Barry Green and Timothy Gallwey, I am going to amend their "Performance Formula" by adding another key ingredient – the *"a"* – Attitude. Making the formula now:

$$P = p + a - i$$

PERFORMANCE = potential plus attitude minus interference

Let's use this equation and apply it to the world of competitive choral competitions as an example. We tend to spend most of our energy and time trying to improve our skills mastery or potential *(our "p")* so that we can score better in competitions in the four judging categories – Sound, Music, Expression and Showmanship. We spend hours of rehearsal, and countless

---

6 Barry Green and W. Timothy Gallwey, *The Inner Game of Music* (Doubleday, New York, 1986) p. 12

dollars, on expert musical coaches to explore every chord and every musical phrase for musical possibility. In the world of Sweet Adeline barbershop harmony a cappella choruses, we frequently spend an entire weekend "retreat," and over 16 hours of singing, working with a musical coach on mastering the technical details and improving our *"p"* for the two songs that we plan on singing at competition.

Imagine, if you will, 100+ women standing on risers in a nondescript hotel ballroom somewhere miles from their hometown singing two songs with intense concentration and high energy for an *entire* weekend. I remember attempting to explain that scenario to a friend once and he thought I was completely nuts.

That is just one example of how our chorus focused on technical mastery – to maximize our potential (our *"p"*). Certainly, that kind of intense focus on skill development is critical for advancement in any skill-based activity. Indeed, in high-level competition there is absolutely no substitution for technical mastery, but that is only one variable in the equation.

Hand in hand with our potential and our skill is our attitude (our *"a"*). Our mental attitude and belief can totally drive our behavior and either enhance our *"p"* or detract from it. I will address how to develop a positive mental attitude for more performance success in Chapter Four.

For now, let's look at the other key part of the performance equation: the interference (the *"i"*). If we work on reducing the stuff that gets in our way, the interference in our lives (the *"i"*), at the same time as we are working to improve our technical mastery (the *"p"*), and developing our positive mental attitude (the *"a"*), we will come closer to achieving our peak performance (the **"P"**).

Olympic swimmer Michael Phelps, eight time gold medalist at the 2008 Summer Olympics in Beijing, has a rigid pre-race routine to empty his mind of all interference and focus on the task at hand. His coach, Bob Bowman, is reported to have said that he thinks that Phelps' greatest strength is psychological.[7] When asked whether, when he pushed off from the pool's edge, he was exhaling or holding his breath underwater, Phelps is quoted as saying that

7   Reprinted from the Washington Post, Aug. 9, 2008

he didn't know, as he doesn't think about anything when he swims. He just gets in the water and races.[8]

Imagine – in extreme conditions of both external and internal interferences – with crowds screaming, whistles blowing, with TV cameras, heat, water (not to mention the incredible pressure of being in an Olympic competition) the world record-holder for winning the most gold medals in a single Olympic Games is able to empty his mind completely of all interference.

How can we reduce interference? How can we filter out the barrage of stuff that surrounds us and manage to focus entirely on what we are doing in the moment?

---

8 Reprinted from the Orange County Register, Aug. 7, 2008

INTERFERENCE REDUX

EXTERNAL INTERFERENCE AWARENESS

It is important to become aware and acknowledge all of the possible things that can throw you off track and take you away from being focused and present.

Becoming aware of external interferences is Step One. Many of the external interferences in our lives we cannot control directly. It is our reaction to these things that decides how much the interferences impact us. The good news is: we *do* have control over our reaction and our own response to these interferences. Do you feel better now?

Have some fun with the "Interference Identification Exercise" on page 18. On the left hand side of the grid, list the external interferences that can get in the way or distract you from achieving your performance potential:

Some examples to get you started:
- ✓ Health issues
- ✓ Traffic
- ✓ Overweight
- ✓ Unfit
- ✓ Not enough time
- ✓ Technology
- ✓ TV

On the right hand side of the grid, list the effect that those interferences have on your performance:

For example:
- ✓ External Interference: Unfit
  Effect: I just don't have the energy to move ahead
- ✓ External Interference : Technology
  Effect: I am constantly distracted and taken off task by my emails

Let's get specific to a Chorus rehearsal and acknowledge any other external interferences that you can imagine and the effect of those interferences on you.

EXTERNAL INTERFERENCE IDENTIFICATION EXERCISE

External Interference List	Effect of that interference
1.	
2.	
3.	
4.	
5.	
6.	
7.	
8.	
9.	
10.	

For example:
- ✓ Interference: Squeakiness of the risers
  Effect: Takes me out of my performance story
- ✓ Interference: Talking on the risers
  Effect: Distracts me and I lose focus

Remember – we are aiming for ways to maximize your own personal performance potential in whatever situation you find yourself, be it a chorus performance or competition, on the job, while playing sports, during an important presentation or in your relationships. We are looking for ways to reduce external interference in the moment so you can continue on the path to your personal peak performance.

EXTERNAL INTERFERENCE REDUX STRATEGIES

Strategy # 1: Notice, Acknowledge, Ignore

When you encounter an external interference in the moment, I recommend you do like the Zen Buddhists do: "Turn your head to it, nod in its direction, then turn your head and ignore it."

In other words, consciously acknowledge the distraction or interference. Give a big old nod in its direction, and then just as consciously turn your head and ignore it. **"Notice, Acknowledge, Ignore."**

The key is to acknowledge it. When one tries to ignore the interference without acknowledging it, it just gives more energy to the interference and it magnifies. Now don't get me wrong. If the air conditioning unit is sounding like an airplane on take-off, then fix it, but if it is neither the time nor within your control to fix it, then do like the Zen Buddhists: "notice" the distraction, "acknowledge" the distraction and then make a conscious decision to "ignore" the distraction.

Let's go back to our air conditioning example. The director notices that her members are fanning themselves with their music on the risers as the heat increases, so she stops and says, "Okay – it is bloomin' hot in here. Let's acknowledge that. It is hot, and it is not going to get any cooler because the A/C is broken. Let's think cool, and continue on. Does that work for everyone?" What she has done in that instance is acknowledge and validate the interference, and then make a conscious decision to get buy-in to carry on with rehearsal under those conditions. Yes, it will be hot still, but by acknowledging the distraction, she leaves no reason for anyone to keep on talking or thinking about it.

If you can master the art of being able to stay present and perform at your best with external interferences, you are well on the way to living your performance potential.

Strategy # 2: The Power of Focus

Here's another technique for eliminating interference, getting focused and bringing you to the present. Use this anywhere, anytime. Use this before walking in the door of your house after a stressful commute; use this before a job interview, or a meeting you are leading; use this before entering the rehearsal hall. You will find you can easily get yourself back on track quickly and focused on the present with the following Three Breath Focus technique.

Three Breath Focus Technique:

When you take these breaths, think about clearing the space right from your feet through your core area and up, (See Chapter Five), feel free to use your arms. As you breathe in, take a big nostrils-flared breath... breathe from your belly (a deep breath that fills you up) and as you release the breath, feel free to vocalize.

When you are familiar with this exercise, you may find it helpful to close your eyes and therefore eliminate another sense so that you can increase the focus. First, I would like you to think of all of the stuff that happened before today that is in your head. Yup, I mean all the stuff that has already happened that you can't do anything to reverse, issues that may be unresolved or things on your "To Do" list that have been there for a while. Turn your active attention to those things.

Now turn your mind to today. Think of everything that happened today: sleeping through your alarm, the hassles at work, the guy that cut you off in traffic, the dinner you burnt, the fight with your teen, your crying baby.

Now consciously think about everything you have to do tomorrow: the deadline you need to meet, the presentation you need to give, the things that worry you.

We are now going to take three deep breaths, and with each breath release and clear our minds of the yesterdays, today and the tomorrows so that we can simply be 100% present right now.

Let's take our first breath. Inhale your yesterdays deeply from your belly and exhale. As you exhale, release all of the thoughts of yesterday.

Let's take our second breath. Inhale your today deeply, and as you exhale, release all of your thoughts of the things that happened today.

Let's take our third breath. Inhale your tomorrows deeply and release those thoughts of your tomorrows.

Relax and breathe deeply and rejoice in being present. You have chosen to give yourself the gift of focus – the gift of being 100% present right now.

INTERNAL INTERFERENCE – SILENCING YOUR INNER CRITIC

Shut the Duck Up!

I am sure we all have one or more voices in our heads that talk to us on a regular basis. Sometimes there is one voice, sometimes several. Frequently, the voice (often referred to as our "inner critic") is nagging, belittling, angry, scolding and generally makes us feel lousy. That voice can shred our chances for growth and happiness faster and more effectively than any external interference.

I call those voices in my head my "ducks" because they are constantly "quack, quack, quacking." Man, they can get loud! You may have one duck or you may have several. Your duck may look like someone specific (your dad, your teacher…) or your duck may just be – well… a duck! Feathered, annoying and loud.

When I do my inner coaching work with groups, I give each person a plastic toy duck so that in the process of our work – if they start hearing quack, quack, quacking in their own heads, they can simply look at their duck and *"Shut the Duck Up!"* [9]

I have been amazed at how this simple concept has resonated with people. What started as a technique to bring awareness to the distracting voices which might get in the way as I did some coaching work that was outside some people's comfort zones, turned into a tool many use in their day-to-day lives. Now, when they hear the quacking, they can smile and simply admit, "Oh, my ducks are quacking big time." You guessed it! As soon as they do this, their ducks shut up!

> *"I do a lot of traveling and speaking to large groups. My duck is packed in my briefcase and travels with me. Shutting my duck up has become part of my pre-speech routine."* – D.R.

> *"I used my duck to give me more confidence as I went in and asked my boss for a raise. Effectively, I made my duck my boss, so was able to role-play and go through and refute all of my boss' arguments before I even entered his office!"* – P.D. (p.s. "I got the raise!")

---

9   Special thanks to Marjorie Busse for use of her concept "Shut the Duck Up!"

IDENTIFICATION OF INTERNAL INTERFERENCES

You will begin to recognize "awareness" as a theme in this book. Awareness is key to the management of our emotional and mental states. Being aware of and acknowledging the kinds of internal interferences that get in our way is the first step toward being able to minimize their adverse effect on us.

Use the following exercise to identify what internal interferences you feel in your life and how they get in the way of you achieving your performance potential.

For example:
- ✓ Internal interference: Lack of self-confidence
  Effect: Limits my choices in social situations
- ✓ Internal interference: Fear of failure
  Effect: Makes me play small

INTERNAL INTERFERENCE IDENTIFICATION EXERCISE

Internal Interference List	Effect of That Interference
1.	
2.	
3.	
4.	
5.	
6.	
7.	
8.	
9.	
10.	

DUCK CONVERSATIONS

When you are about to do something and your duck starts quacking, there probably isn't a lot of time to have a dialogue or argue with your duck. In those moments you just have to "Shut the Duck Up!" When you do have time for a conversation with your duck, I would like you to consider that the quacking you hear loud and clear is only part of what your duck wants to tell you. It just happens to be the loudest part of what your duck wants to say.

If you can think of your duck's quacking as a P.A. (Possibility Announcement), you can learn a lot by digging deeper to find out what that possibility is. Much like the booming announcement that comes over a Public Address System (a P.A.), your duck's quacking is loud and sometimes incomprehensible. A probing conversation with your duck may well unearth the gems of new possibilities.

If we take the bottom line premise that your duck loves you and really wants the best for you, then we begin to perceive the quacking much differently. If you can be still long enough, and persist in asking your duck what it is really trying to say, you can reap great information and support.

Lisa tried this technique when she got home after facilitating a workshop and critically started analyzing her performance. "Quack, quack, quack," said her duck. "You didn't allow enough time for the exercises. You were talking too quickly. The room set up was awkward. People were confused. Quack, quack, quack."

"Shut the Duck up!" said Lisa. "If you are just going to be negative and criticize me I am not going to listen. Tell me then – what can I do differently next time to make my workshop better?"

Lo and behold… the deafening quacking quieted and her duck began to tell her ideas that she could work on to make her workshop better the next time. "Maybe you could rethink the amount of material you try to cover in the workshop so you don't have to rush as much," said her duck.

"Good point," said Lisa, "what else?"

" I think you need to get to the workshop site earlier so that you can make sure you have the room set up to allow for the exchanges you want" said her duck.

"Thanks," said Lisa… and so on. Lisa was well on the way to improving her performance potential – with the help of her duck!

When you do have the time to question your duck, I encourage you to challenge it for the answers, for the advice, and for the encouragement and coaching that it can give you once the annoying quacking quiets down.

YOUR DUCK AS YOUR LIFETIME ALLY

Your duck is your friend. For one thing, your duck is always there for you just waiting to be asked for his or her advice, help and support. Have you been calling on your duck for anything?

Donna used her plastic toy duck to help her get through her first Chemotherapy treatment. She describes how she was quite nervous despite the unbelievable support she had from friends and family and the gifts and messages they gave her for good energy. For good luck she packed in her bag several stuffed bears and survivor symbols, her International Competition chorus medal, and photos of her loved ones. As an afterthought, Donna grabbed her duck from her desk and threw it in her purse.

She said, "Good thing I did. I started having a panic attack as we were nearing the hospital. Having my duck with me and being able to grab it as I reached into my purse to shut up those voices definitely made me ready for whatever the chemo experience would bring. I carried that duck in my hand all the way to the treatment bed where it stayed with me for the entire six-hour session. My duck also accompanied me to each of my four chemo treatments and 33 radiation treatments. She never left my side, always reminding me to think and act positively and that I am loved and surrounded by the love and strength of many."

Imagine having a friend there whenever you need one. It worked for Donna and it can work for you, too. Use the following exercise to help turn your duck into your greatest ally.

EXERCISE:
TURNING YOUR DUCK INTO YOUR GREATEST ALLY

What is your duck saying to you when it quacks?

What is the possibility announcement? (Why do you think your duck is saying that to you?)

If you believe that your duck is the greatest ally and friend, what does your duck really want for you?

What does your duck say when you then ask it for specific steps to help you?

3

WHY NOT?
Eliminating Your Limiting Beliefs

A LIMITING BELIEF: a previously held assumption
that gets in the way of you moving forward thus
limiting the possibilities for any situation

I am betting that everyone reading this has experienced first-hand the effects of having limiting beliefs about his or her life. Maybe those limiting beliefs prevented you from pursuing a new job, a new adventure, or even a new relationship. Where on earth do those limiting beliefs come from? How did they pop into your head, and how can you reframe them so they do not have an adverse effect on your life's possibilities?

Some of our limiting beliefs were taught to us, some were modeled for us by our elders, and some we learned or picked up by osmosis. Some were arrived at by as little as one simple off-hand comment from a teacher or a sibling, years earlier. We then attached importance to that comment, gave energy to it, and that limiting belief then became our truth, and as the years went by, became real for us.

For instance, I am consistently astounded by the number of people who say, "I can't sing." This is often a limiting belief arrived at by a comment levied at them at some point in their childhood. Believe it or not, back in the dark ages when I was in Grade One, we were labeled and assigned to groups according to how well we could sing. It was terrifying as the Music Teacher walked around the room from person to person with her ear cocked listening to us sing. Each student was then given the name of a bird that represented their singing ability. Their name was printed on a paper cutout of that particular bird and put up on the wall for the entire year for all to see. Thankfully, I got grouped with the "canaries," but what about the poor kids who got labeled as "crows"? I am pretty sure they are the ones in adulthood saying, "Oh no, I can't sing." How sad to think that a limiting belief might keep anyone from doing something that could bring him or her joy and happiness.

It is common to have negative beliefs or limiting beliefs around a big stretch goal or a situation that might take us out of our Comfort Zone.

"Oh no," you say, " I am way too old to run a marathon."
"Oh no," you say, "I am not smart enough, talented enough, don't have enough experience to do that job!"
"Oh no," you say, "I am not a good enough singer to sing in a quartet."
"Oh no," you say, "I am too old to find a love relationship."

How easy it is to create safety for ourselves by staying in a place where we feel comfortable, a place we know. Our limiting beliefs, in a sense, protect us from getting hurt. "So," you may say, "aren't those limiting beliefs a good thing then?" Well sure, if you never want to do anything or try anything that makes you in the least bit uncomfortable or about which you have any doubts, but in the unknown lies the amazing world of possibility.

When we examine our limiting beliefs closely we find that they are rarely true, or, we don't really have any idea if they are true or not but for some reason we just blithely take them at face value and believe them. What if we started listening to our "unlimiting beliefs" instead?

My client Meredith, who was in the throes of a mid-life transition, found that she could easily write a long list of limiting beliefs around pretty much every facet of her life. We worked at turning those limiting beliefs into unlimiting beliefs instead. An admitted workaholic, one of Meredith's limiting beliefs was that if you were working at a high level, it was virtually impossible to have balance in your life.

When we started our coaching process, Meredith was working ten hour days, six days a week, in a high-level, demanding position.

She had resigned herself to a life of either work and no life… or no work and some kind of life balance. Working from that place, her life prospects were severely limited.

When she reframed that belief to an affirmation that she could work at a high level *and* create balance in her life, the possibilities opened up for her. Through our coaching together, she realized that the issues were not with the level of the position she held or the company she worked for, they were with her current work habits and lack of boundaries between her work and personal life. Those were areas that were possible for her to change and she has embraced the challenges with zeal.

As we move forward to achieve our goals, we can choose to hold on to our limiting beliefs and then bust our butts trying to move forward, resisted by the huge headwind of our limiting beliefs, or we can choose to first get rid of our limiting mental beliefs and then fly with a huge tailwind and get to our destination a lot faster and easier.

For example: Let's say you want to sing in a quartet, but deep down inside you have a limiting belief that "I will never be a good enough singer to sing in a quartet." You rehearse and rehearse, take vocal lessons, and "try" quartetting and you do improve, however, as long as you still believe that "I will never be a good enough singer to sing in a quartet," you will limit the possibilities for growth and definitely slow down your progress. Chances are your quartet experience will be less fun, less fulfilling and only temporary. How much easier it would be to let the limiting belief go and then work toward becoming the best singer you can be.

The mind is a powerful force, as you will discover as you continue to read this book. Use your incredible mind for good, not evil! Use your mind to harness the brilliance inside and your infinite life possibilities instead of letting your mind limit your greatness.

EXERCISE:
TURNING A LIMITING BELIEF
INTO A POWERFUL POSSIBILITY

1. Write down a stretch goal in any area of your life: e.g., "I want to run a marathon."

2. State your limiting belief(s) around that stretch goal: e.g., "I am way too old to run a marathon."

3. True or False? Assess the truth of your limiting belief(s) statement. "Has anyone my age ever run a marathon before?" (you might have to google that one!) "Is it physically *possible* to run a marathon at my age?"

4. Determine the "What if?" possibility: e.g., "If I am not too old to run a marathon, what would I do? What could I do? What are the possibilities for me?"

5. Re-frame your Limiting Belief from question 2: e.g., "I am physically capable of running a marathon."

6. Embrace the Possibility: Once you have determined that your limiting belief is not true, decide to change it. Once you have determined it is possible, determine what you need to do to begin to move toward your stretch goal: e.g., "If I really want to run a marathon I need to create a comprehensive and realistic training plan that I can stick to."

7. Live into the possibility and create an action plan using S.M.A.R.T. Goals (see Chapter 9).

   MY ACTION PLAN:

   Celebrate!

ALL HAIL THE SHREDDER!
REFRAMING LIMITING BELIEFS

One of the favorite things I do in my inner coaching work with leadership teams is an exercise to reframe the team's limiting beliefs around a project goal. In any team situation, if the leaders have limiting beliefs around their stated goals, they need to be identified, reframed and eliminated. An issue or problem that is obvious, but which is ignored by a group of people, generally out of embarrassment or taboo or fear of conflict, is often referred to as the "Elephant in the Room." The theory is based on the idea that an elephant in a room would be impossible to overlook; thus, people in the room who pretend the elephant is not there might be concerning themselves with relatively small and even irrelevant matters, compared to the looming big one. These elephants, or limiting beliefs, if left unexpressed and not dealt with, can totally sabotage any goal. The leadership has a huge impact on the rest of the team and if they do not believe in a goal, it will not happen.

When working with the teams, the first step I take is to check in with the team to make sure that everyone is clear and in agreement about what the team or project goal is. Without clarity and consensus on where they want to go, it is nearly impossible to move forward.

I then go around the room and have each member of the team identify their limiting belief about the project goal. I ask the person to write down on a brightly colored piece of paper what that limiting belief is. They hold on to the paper until everyone has stated their limiting beliefs. After all of the limiting beliefs are completely exhausted (and some people may have several limiting beliefs), we then do the second part of the exercise.

I put a paper shredder in the center of the room and each person again reads out their limiting belief and then figures out a way to reframe that belief to the positive and then says the reframed belief aloud. After they tell the team the reframe, they ceremoniously run that old limiting belief through the paper shredder. "Grrrrrr!" the shredder grinds it to pieces and it is gone! This can be a lengthy exercise and is not always pleasant. Listening to each team member's inner limiting beliefs can be a tough thing to experience at times, however, if the team stays open and non-judgmental, when the belief finally gets reframed and shredded, it is cathartic and opens up a world of possibility for both the individual and the team.

At a Music Leadership retreat I facilitated for the Song of Atlanta Chorus, we had the privilege of holding the retreat at Connie's beach home in Florida. We did not have access to a shredder, so instead, as each person reframed their limiting beliefs for the chorus goals for the 2008 International Competition in Hawaii, they ripped up the brightly colored pieces of paper and threw them on the floor in the middle of the room. What an amazing visual!

As the pile of shredded limitations grew we decided to leave them on the floor in the center of the room as we continued our inner coaching workshop for the rest of the weekend as a reminder to stay open to possibility. It was a very effective visual for everyone as they had to step over, walk on, wade through and observe these "shredded limitations."

We lived with those shredded beliefs scattered ceremoniously over the floor for a good 18 hours before the orderly baritones in the room finally caved... and had to clean up the mess on our final evening!

A chorus leadership team I worked with took well over two hours to declare all of their limiting beliefs around their chorus' competition goal and then reframe them. Another chorus leadership team danced around the real elephant for a long time before someone finally felt the safety and trust of the group and could put it on the table. Clearly, identifying and then getting rid of these elephants is key to being able to move forward.

The meeting note taker records only the "reframed" beliefs, and distributes them after the meeting, thus creating a working manifesto with which the group can move forward.

Imagine how doing this exercise with your team before embarking on a project could serve to clarify and unify the group and head many potential project roadblocks off at the pass.

A common limiting belief with a high-level chorus is for a leader not to believe that everyone in the group is working at a championship level of commitment. One chorus I worked with had a section leader whose limiting belief was: "I think that the others in my section aren't working as hard as I am and aren't really committed to doing the work they need to do to improve their voices to get to the next level." It took a long time for that section leader to really understand that by holding that belief, she was, in fact, destroying the possibility for growing toward excellence. When she finally reframed her limiting belief and threw it in the shredder, she said, "I trust that my section is doing whatever they can each individually do to become better singers and I will do everything that I can to ensure that they have the tools and the motivation to get better." Instantly, the world of possibility opened up for her and her section.

REMOVING THE LIMITING BARRIERS TO POSSIBILITY

NO BLOCKING

Many of you will be familiar with the TV show *Whose Line is it Anyway?* or, with improvisational theatre like *Theatresports* where two people are creating theatre on the spot with no script. In improvisational theatre, one of the prime rules is "no blocking," which means you must not deny or "block" a suggestion or a question from your partner because if you do, it immediately squelches the possibilities and kills the scene. Blocking is the opposite of saying "Yes."

Here are a couple of examples of blocking. Notice how they stop the movement forward and effectively kill the scene.

Player One: "I'll give you $10 for that chicken."
Player Two: "No." (Player One is shut down.)

or

Player Two: Holds up a ball from the prop chest.
Player One says: "I'll give you $10 for that chicken."
Player Two: "This isn't a chicken! It's a ball." (Again, Player Two threw up a block. What if Player Two had played along with the ball being the chicken? Imagine the possibilities for the scene.)

Think about this in the context of your life. What words and phrases shut down possibility and creative thinking? Has this ever happened to you? Were you ever blocked: perhaps when you threw out an idea in a staff meeting, or perhaps when in a conversation with a colleague?

More importantly, have you ever blocked someone? Imagine a life where there was "No Blocking." Imagine the possibilities that would remain alive!

BUT I HAVE ALWAYS DONE IT THIS WAY!

A husband and wife were preparing dinner one night, and before they put the ham in the oven to cook, the wife cut off both ends of the ham. The husband asked her "Why do you always cut off both ends of the ham before cooking it?" She replied, "That's how my mom cooked it." Well, it just so happened that her mom was coming over for dinner that night so they asked her, "Why did you always cut off both ends of the ham?" Mom replied, "That's how my mom cooked it." They decided to call Grandma on the phone and ask her why she cut off the ends of the ham. Her answer? "Because my pan was too small!"[10]

Aha! Doing something without questioning it because has always been done that way... is there anything that you have been doing that doesn't make sense but "it has always been done that way?" Uttering the eight words, "... but we have always done it this way..." is a sure fire way to stifle creativity and eliminate possibility.

Think about it: Where have *you* been cutting the ends off the ham???

---

10 T. Harv Eker, *Secrets of the Millionaire Mind* (New York: Harper Collins, 2005) p. 26

EXERCISE: CREATING POSSIBILITIES

e.g., **Action:** Commuting to work
    Way I have always done it: Freeway
    New possibilities: Leave early and take the back roads
    New possible results: Less stress, might enjoy the
commute more

Action	Way I Have Always Done It	New Possible Choices	New Possible Results

WHY NOT?

"The greatest danger for most of us is not that our aim is too high and we miss it, but that it is too low and we reach it."

– Michelangelo

How often do we limit our thinking by playing too small? Remember the movie *ROCKY*? The story of a small-time, struggling boxer working in a meat factory who had a dream of making the big time by fighting against the world heavyweight champion, Apollo Creed, struck a chord in all of us. I remember leaving the movie theatre after the first screening of *Rocky* so hyped up, that along with a good portion of the audience, I shadowboxed my way down the street. The story of someone who believed in the possibilities, who thought big and made it happen, was inspirational.

I remember back to the 2007 International a cappella chorus competition when, after the semi-final round of competition, the 12th ranked Lions Gate Chorus achieved our goal of making the Top Ten. Word on the street was that people even thought we could be in the Top Five! Wow! Not in our wildest imagination did we ever consider that possibility. The scores in the International Competition are cumulative and we had two days to rehearse before the chorus finals competition. As we rehearsed we began to ask ourselves, "Why not? Why limit our thinking? Maybe we could make the Top Five? Why not?" As a group we collectively decided that we would be open to all possibilities.

The finals day came and we were calm and confident with the full belief in our potential, in the possibility. We performed our fifteen-minute finals package once again to the screams and standing ovation of the crowd. Were we surprised when they announced Lions Gate Chorus as 3rd place Bronze Medalists? You betcha! We had exceeded our wildest expectations. In the world of high-level a cappella competition, we had done the unheard of: jumped from 12th place ranking to a 3rd place finish out of 600 choruses worldwide.

What if we had limited our thinking? What if we had ruled out the possibility of getting in the Top Five? What if we hadn't said, "Why not?"

Use the exercise on page 40 to explore your thinking of the "Why not?" stretch possibilities. Pick an action, create a goal and then dream of a stretch possibility. I encourage you to think big; in your own life and for your friends, family and colleagues. Keep the possibilities open so that your (and their) greatness can shine. Why not?

EXERCISE: WHY NOT?

e.g., Using the example on page 38:

Action: Compete in the International Competition
The Possibility: Get in the Top Ten
The Why Not? Stretch Possibility: Get in the Top Five

Action	The Possibility	The Why Not? Stretch Possibility

4

POLLYANNA LIVES!
The Power of Positive Thinking

"Keep your face in the sunshine and you can never see the shadow."

– Helen Keller

Remember the story of Pollyanna – the child heroine of the children's classic 1913 novel by Eleanor H. Porter? Pollyanna's philosophy of life centered on, what she called, the "Glad Game," which consisted of finding something about which to be glad in every situation. Pollyanna was orphaned, and as a young girl was forced to go and live in a dispirited small town in Vermont with her ruthlessly stern Aunt Polly. With her infectiously sunny personality and her "Glad Game" philosophy, Pollyanna gradually transformed the grumpy town, its inhabitants and even her horrid Aunt Polly, to a life of optimism and happiness. I once had the "Oh you are such a Pollyanna" comment leveled at me as some sort of insult for being foolishly or illogically optimistic. I chose to receive that as a compliment instead. Wouldn't the world be a better place if there were more Pollyannas? Pollyanna may have only changed a small town, but couldn't a whole city or country begin to be transformed if more of us adopted positive attitudes and started playing the "Glad Game?"

Besides the mental health benefits of approaching life positively, it is important to remember that our thoughts and emotions are completely intertwined with our physical selves. Researchers have proven that maintaining a positive attitude will help give you a longer, healthier life.

Certainly it has been medically proven that all sorts of physical ailments and disease have been brought on by negative mental attitudes and stress.

We have all felt the effects on our emotional well being that the projection of someone else's attitude can bring to us. Have you ever gone out for a social evening and returned home exhausted, not by the hours of dancing, but by the company you kept? Conversely, have you ever hung up the phone completely hyper and energized by a phone conversation you had?

Our attitudes drive our behavior. By enhancing our positive mental attitude we protect our own personal energy field, and as our minds move to a new, healthy way of being, so will our lives.

CREATING POSITIVITY ZONES

Creating a positivity zone may be one of the easiest and most effective things that you ever do for your mental health. It simply involves an intentional decision to make a particular physical area of your life a positivity zone.

Choose the place and the space and enroll your constituents! Your positivity zone could be your office, your car, your living room or you could create several positivity zones. Your positivity zone becomes a sacred place. You might even want to put up signage to remind everyone that it is a positivity zone.

Kay and her partner turned their bedroom into a positivity zone so that there was at least one room in the house where there was a definite cutoff from daily hassles. They look forward to that time away from stress, and even walking into the room makes them feel more peaceful. They sleep better and wake up without any of the former nagging thoughts of negative stuff that "needs" to be dealt with.

We regularly declare our chorus rehearsal hall a positivity zone because keeping the chorus' mind in a positive space creates increased opportunity for growth and learning. It is amazing how the group then takes ownership and will remind others of the positivity zone if they start going down a negativity path during rehearsal.

One night our director arrived late to chorus rehearsal after her long commute and launched into the story of her car troubles and traffic woes and near traffic accident. She was visibly stressed out and you could see the chorus members (as compassionate, caring women) all feeling worse and more badly for her as the story continued. Luckily someone interrupted her rant and pointed out loudly, "Well, thank heavens you have now entered a positivity zone." The group chuckled heartily, and the director realized that she had gone down a sorry path that wasn't going to serve her or the rehearsal. It was a lovely moment as she said laughingly, "Oh drat – that damn positivity zone"… and then reframed and continued the rehearsal in a positive vein.

Enroll support from your family, co-workers or friends in the creation and respect of your positivity zone. It is much easier having others buy into the same way of being. Make your quartet rehearsal a positivity zone, or your staff meeting, or your family dinner conversation. Allow for permission to give each other reminders should someone venture into a "downward spiral" of conversation.

Every day Rachelle endured a vanpool for 1.5 hours into her job in Los Angeles with a co-rider we will call "Negative Nancy" (NN). For 1.5 hours in the morning and 1.5 hours every evening (frequently longer in traffic) she was subject to a torrent of negativity and a barrage of complaints about pretty much any subject in the universe. There seemed to be no end to the things that bothered NN! By the time she got home at night, Rachelle was absolutely exhausted. The most she ever felt like doing was opening a bottle of wine and watching some mindless reality TV show. Rachelle felt like there was a lot of stuff she really wanted to do when she got home and in her life but was just too exhausted.

Rachelle decided that she had to designate the van a positivity zone in order to aid in her mental preparation for the weeks leading up to the International Chorus competition in Hawaii. Rachelle enlisted the support of Negative Nancy. She explained that she was in training for the "Olympics of Singing" and had to prepare mentally very seriously and that creating a "van positivity zone" would really help her out. As soon as the van became a positivity zone, Rachelle's life shifted. Not only was she in a better mood when she arrived at work, but she also had an amazing amount of energy when she arrived home at night. A social life started, and Rachelle had begun to explore the things that she really wanted to do in her spare time but had simply been too tired to begin before. Rachelle later spoke to me in tears as she relayed her story. "Creating a positivity zone in the van literally changed my life!" she gushed.

(I can't help but think that Negative Nancy felt some positive transformational shifts in her life as well.)

REFLECTION QUESTIONS

1. How easy would it be to transform your home or workplace into a positivity zone?

2. Who could you enlist for support?

3. What difference could creating a positivity zone make for you?

SWITCHING TO THE POSITIVE SELF-TALK CHANNEL

What thoughts are you thinking that are dragging you down and holding you back? Could you give yourself a gift by grabbing the remote and tuning in to a different self-talk channel? You can change your old negative programming and create new neural pathways by taking charge of your thoughts and adopting new positive thoughts. Negative self-talk will make you feel unmotivated, tired and even physically ill.

Keeping yourself in a positive frame of mind is not always easy when the world and others conspire to take you out of that, but there are some powerful ways you can easily tune back in to the positive self-talk channel.

1. Choose your thoughts carefully

Check in with yourself to see what negative messaging you are giving yourself. "I am too fat," "I don't think I can do that," "I will never have enough money to get out of debt," "Life is hard," "This town sucks," or perhaps those gems we hear often during chorus life like "I am a klutz – I will never get this choreography right," "I will never have enough breath to make it through that phrase," "I could never sing in a quartet." Awareness of what we are thinking is the first step, so learn to listen to your words, whether unspoken or spoken.

Once you notice the dialogue you are having with yourself, think about the choice you can make – either to stay with the debilitating thoughts, or to choose a different thought. It *is* your choice. Inspirational best-selling author Louise Hay said, "You are the only thinker in your own mind." We cannot control what others think, but we can choose our own thoughts. Create the thoughts you want.

2. Focus on today

Take a deep breath and release your thoughts from old memories and hurts that no longer serve you. Take another deep breath and release your thoughts about the uncertainties and the "What will I do tomorrow?" Stay with the present. Find joy in what you have in your life today. Live the moments you have today.

As I grew up, my summers were spent happily at the Ottawa YWCA Camp Davern, near Perth, Ontario. It was a camp tradition for all campers to meet and line up at the flagpole each morning before breakfast to recite the Salutation to the Dawn in unison as a reminder to the girls ages 8-16 to live and be present in this moment – what a beautiful concept.

Look to this day!
For it is life, the very life of life.
In its brief course
Lie all the verities and realities of your existence:

The bliss of growth
The glory of action
The splendor of beauty

For yesterday is but a dream
And tomorrow only a vision
But today well-lived makes every yesterday a dream of happiness
And every tomorrow a vision of hope.
Look well, therefore to this day.
Such is the Salutation to the Dawn

– Kalidasa, poet, from ancient Sanskrit

3. Focus on what *you* can do

Focus on what you can do to contribute to a better world and not what you expect others to do, nor what you think others expect you to do. Let go of expectations about how things "should be." In fact, why don't you just throw out the "shoulds" completely and embrace the "coulds" instead? As you focus on positive possibilities, you'll find that positive energy follows.

EXERCISE:
SWITCHING TO A POSITIVE SELF-TALK CHANNEL

1. Who in your life is a positive, energy-giving force? (It is said we are the average of the five people with whom we spend the most time.)

2. Who do you spend time with who is actively on a path of moving forward and making their lives better?

3. What things do you do to nurture yourself physically, emotionally, spiritually and intellectually?

4. What damaging habits do you have that aren't working for you anymore?

5. What are you holding onto that is no longer serving you? (e.g., old emails from a work disagreement, old hurts from a long-ago personal disagreement, the pants you wore in high school that you think you might fit into again). What would it take for you to let those things go?

Sally is a feisty southern belle of-a-certain-age with an incredible depth of life experiences, knowledge and interests. Over the years, Sally had found herself getting increasingly drawn into negative conversations and consequently dragged down by them. Sally had experienced some recent losses and life changes which had opened her up to questioning her life direction and where she was placing her considerable energy.

After participating in an inner coaching weekend retreat that I ran with a music leadership team of which Sally was a part, her attitude shifted to one of positivity. She had been involved in a task force for a nature center that had been fraught with problems, and Sally had been frustrated and about to resign. By shifting to a positive, appreciative mindset, Sally suddenly felt re-energized, more positive and a much more productive member of the task force.

The bottom line for Sally was that a positive influence in one part of her life couldn't help spilling over and having an exponential effect on other parts of her life. Sally said she felt like "I have shed a skin and there is a shiny new person there!"

Like Sally, you too can shift your life and begin to accentuate the positive by putting some energy around a change of attitude.

SEVEN STRATEGIES FOR POSITIVE-IZING YOUR LIFE

STRATEGY # 1: Exit gracefully

Remove yourself from all negative conversations and/or situations as quickly as possible. When your co-worker starts to whine about the wrongs of the world, do not engage. Change the subject, reframe, say something positive and walk away. Whiners and complainers will usually shut up if they are not getting you to buy into their complaints.

STRATEGY # 2: Enlist Support

Enlist the support of your family and co-workers. Tell them that you are trying to see what the effects of a positive attitude might have on your life and success, and need them to support you. (Hey, you never know, your positive attitude might be contagious!)

STRATEGY # 3: Change the channel

Turn off the TV news and definitely do not listen to the news before bedtime. Those grim messages you receive right before sleeping will stay with you and amplify through the night.

STRATEGY # 4: Be grateful

Spend five minutes, just before you fall asleep, writing down what of value happened or what you noticed that day for which you are grateful. You will find that you will begin to be more aware of and thankful for the small things (the little girl next door who smiled at you), small victories (like getting the Christmas tree lights untangled) as well as the bigger things (I am grateful that I am warm in my bed with a roof over my head in this Vancouver monsoon). You will go to sleep with positive thoughts rather than worried and stressful thoughts.

STRATEGY # 5: Feed Yourself

Surround yourself with reminders of your fabulous-ness. Fill your home, your office, your car, with positive messaging; photos of the people you love, things you love, images or quotes that inspire you. Stay centered and remind yourself that you are a unique being. There is only one you.

STRATEGY # 6: Empty your mind daily

Put aside at least 15 minutes per day for mindful self-care. Do something to slow your thinking mind (the place where all of your fear or negative thoughts exist). What do you like to do that takes you out of your thinking mind? Consciously add in those activities at least once a day, e.g., playing an instrument, laughing, meditating, reciting your affirmation, gardening, going for a walk on the beach or in the park, doing some gratitude journaling, calling a friend who replenishes your energy, listening to music... you choose!

STRATEGY # 7: Distribute Happiness

We know our culture is ridden with constant negative messaging from the media. Combating this culture of doom sometimes takes a heroic Pollyanna-type move. Consciously distributing happiness is a fabulous way of shifting the energy surrounding you to create more joy. Play the Pollyanna Glad Game. See how much happiness you can spread.

END THE AWFUL-IZING

"When you look for the bad expecting it, you will find it."

– from Pollyanna by Eleanor H. Porter

Awful-izing. That's what I call it when we project our worst fears on a situation. The "but what ifs?" can absolutely paralyze you. Someone coined the acronym F.E.A.R. as meaning "False Evidence Appearing Real." The practice of awful-izing creatively dreams up every possible scenario as to what might happen in a situation, taking the results over to the ridiculous.

For example: You are worried about a presentation you have to give to your Board of Directors at work, so you begin to awful-ize. "I am going to be so nervous that I will stand up there and my knees will be knocking and I will forget everything even my name and then I will start to shake and my voice will quaver and I will be so embarrassed that I will burst out crying and run from the room and the Board of Directors will all think I am a total idiot and will fire me on the spot and then I won't be able to get another job and will miss my mortgage payment and be put out on the street and be homeless begging for money outside the liquor store." Whewff!

Do the "End the Awful-izing" exercise on the following page whenever you feel your active imagination begin to take you down a sorry path.

EXERCISE: END THE AWFUL-IZING

1. Describe a situation that worries you.

2. Write down or tell someone all of the things about the situation you are worried might happen. Make sure you get creative and go over the top with your "Awful-izing."

3. Read what you wrote and assess how likely any of your "Awful-izing" predictions are going to happen.

Have a good chuckle and take a deep breath.

CHANGING YOUR THOUGHT DEFAULT

*"Human beings, by changing the inner attitude of their minds,
can change the outer aspect of their lives."*

– William James, American psychologist and author 1842-1910

We all have heard the expression that someone's cup is either half-empty or
half-full. Just as there are two ways to describe the liquid in a cup, there are
also two ways to view anything that happens in our lives and in the world.

WHAT'S THE MRI?

When something does something that you don't like, before you react, consider first what might be the "MRI?" – The Most Respectful Interpretation.[11]
If you give that person, and yourself, the benefit of the doubt and consciously choose the Most Respectful Interpretation, you open the door to
possibility where before there was none.

To give an example, let's say someone speeds by you and then cuts you
off in traffic. Your knee-jerk reaction might be to yell, "What an idiot!,"
and angrily honk your horn and make a rude finger gesture. Your first and
most reactive interpretation might be that he did it on purpose and that he
is trying to run you off the road.

What if you considered your MRI – your Most Respectful Interpretation?
(You do not need to know that this is true, it is just a possibility.)
1. He is trying to get to the hospital in such a hurry because his wife just
    had a baby.
2. He is late for a first date with the woman of his dreams.
3. He is late for a meeting with the president of his company.

Creating an MRI is a *choice*, and by consciously creating an MRI, you create
the possibility of a different outcome.

---

11 A concept from the fertile mind and heart of John J. Scherer, author of *Five Questions that Change
   Everything: Life Lessons at Work*. Used with 'enthusiastic permission'. (He used to sing in a five-person
   folk group in the late 1960s!)

EXERCISE: CHANGING YOUR THOUGHT DEFAULT

Reframe the following statements. What's your MRI? (Most Respectful Interpretation) Notice how your MRI opens up possibilities.

1. He hasn't called me in three days. He must hate me.
   MRI:

2. My boss didn't say good morning today. I must be in trouble.
   MRI:

3. The director glared at me when we just sang that passage. I must have sung something wrong.
   MRI:

4. No one is coming to wait on our table. They are deliberately ignoring us!
   MRI:

POSITIVITY BREEDS POSSIBILITY

"Today is your day, your mountain is waiting, so get on your way."

– Dr. Seuss

THE OPPORTUNITY CLOCK

Personal development and leadership expert, Chris Widener[12], calls our annoying morning alarm clock an "Opportunity Clock." He has taken the one thing that most people dread and changed it into a motivational reminder. Each day is an opportunity for living, learning, loving – a new opportunity to do and to be. The piercing of the alarm clock can be reframed to refer to a positive beginning – a new day of opportunity – of possibility.

GIVE SOMEONE A MULLIGAN

A *mulligan*, in a golf game, refers to a do-over when an errant shot is hit. The practice originally referred to a correction shot on the first tee but over time has very civilly been expanded to include a do-over on any hole. A mulligan gives someone (or yourself) another chance to make it right. Everyone needs at least one mulligan per day.

Next time someone does something thoughtless or something that annoys you, why not give them a mulligan? Give them a do-over. Chances are they didn't do whatever they did on purpose anyway. You will instantly feel better for giving them a break and letting that "bad shot" go! Giving a mulligan opens up a possibility for something better to happen.

CELEBRATING WHAT'S RIGHT WITH THE WORLD

Dewitt Jones, long time National Geographic photographer, has developed a compelling and inspirational training program in which he talks about the philosophy of the National Geographic being to "celebrate what's right with the world, not what's wrong." If we choose to see the beauty, the opportunity, the possibility in any situation – that creates the reality.

---

12 www.chriswidener.com

He talks about how the statement "I won't believe it until I see it" must be turned around to "I won't see it until I believe it." Some of Dewitt's most amazing photos were taken when he adopted that philosophy. As we shift our attitudes, so the world shifts with us.

"As I celebrated what was right with the world, I began to build a vision of possibility, not scarcity. Possibility… always another right answer."

– Dewitt Jones[13]

REFLECTION QUESTIONS

1. What might open up in your life by celebrating what is right in the situation?

2. Does anyone in your life deserve a Mulligan?

3. Where in your life could you shift to "I won't *see* it until I *believe* it"?

5

THE "WOO WOO" PRIMER
Creating a Grounded Foundation

*"You must live in the present, launch yourself on every wave,
and find your eternity in each moment."*

– Henry David Thoreau

Okay, this is the "woo woo" chapter! Consider yourself warned! Living on the West Coast assumes that our more laid-back lives will naturally include some "woo woo" alternative thinking practices. In actual fact, principles such as awareness, mindfulness, centering, grounding and energy work are quite mainstream and have been practiced for years in other arenas, most notably in competitive sports.

Admittedly, I was not convinced of all of this "woo woo" stuff until I saw the results of it evidenced in a dramatically enhanced performance of the 120-voiced championship Lions Gate Chorus, and at the same time felt it working internally with me. I began applying and transferring these "woo woo" principles to other parts of my life. It makes infinite sense and is actually quite simple when you think about it. If you could do anything that would help you feel more grounded, connected, confident, present, open and stress-free, wouldn't you consider it? If you could harness the invisible, yet all-powerful forces of energy within and around you, wouldn't you? Performers, if you could create that magical audience connection that stems from "presence" wouldn't you do it?

NBA's all time greatest basketball coach, Phil Jackson, introduced the concept of "mindful basketball" to many all-stars such as Michael Jordan,

Kobe Bryant and Shaq O'Neill. Jackson wrote a book about his concepts, called *Sacred Hoops*, with techniques that focus on the power of awareness and mindfulness both on and off the court. "When players practice what is known as mindfulness – simply paying attention to what's actually happening – not only do they play better and win more, they also become more attuned with each other. And the joy they experience working in harmony is a powerful motivating force that comes from deep within, not from some frenzied coach pacing along the sidelines, shouting obscenities into the air."[14]

When you are playing at a high level of competition or wanting to "play big," it is critical that you are completely present and aware of everything around you. Just as you can't give a "star" performance on the basketball court if your mind is thinking about past or future events, neither can you give a fabulous connected performance if you are not completely in the moment.

I had the honor of hearing Matthieu Ricard, a Buddhist monk and the French interpreter for the Dalai Lama, speak on our state of consciousness at the 2008 International Coach Federation conference in Montreal. When I contacted Ricard for this book, he generously expanded his words:

> "The primary quality of consciousness is simply knowing, pure awareness. This faculty of knowing underlies every mental event; it is not itself affected by any of these events. This permits us to understand that it is possible to transform the content of our thoughts and experiences."

Ricard left a promising career as a cellular geneticist nearly 40 years ago to study Buddhism in the Himalayas. As a trained scientist and Buddhist monk, he is an active participant in the current scientific research on the effects of meditation on the brain. Mental work, meditation and cultivating inner peace can have incredible clinical implications and Ricard said:

> "The primary goal of meditation is to transform our experience of the world, but it has also been shown that meditation has beneficial effects on our health. For the last ten years, major research centers have been conducting studies on meditation and its long and short-term

---

14 Phil Jackson, *Sacred Hoops* (New York: Hyperion Books, 1995) p. 5

effect on the brain. Experienced meditators are able to generate precise targeted mental states that are enduring and powerful, such as loving-kindness, compassion and emotional balance. A growing number of studies also indicate that meditation considerably reduces stress, anxiety, the tendency toward anger, and the risk of relapse for people who have previously undergone at least two episodes of serious depression. It also significantly strengthens the immune system, reinforces positive emotions, the faculty of attention, and reduces arterial pressure in those suffering from high blood pressure. The study of the influence of our mental states on our health, which was once considered a purely eccentric notion, is now becoming more and more the mainstream approach in scientific research."[15]

Not only will the techniques outlined in this chapter enhance the performance of your group or team, but you can also use this information personally and professionally to make a profound difference in your life.

This "woo woo" chapter is a hybrid compilation of many teachings I have learned in doing my "inner coaching" work with singing groups. I had the good fortune to have had two women in Lions Gate Chorus introduce and teach me many of the principles we will be discussing: Bea is an amazingly spiritual and ageless eighty-three year old woman (just looking into her eyes gives one a sense of solidity and presence), and Vi is a trained Jin Shin Do practitioner and a lifelong believer in the power-of-energy work. Both of these women were talking about this "woo woo" stuff and teaching these concepts to Lions Gate Chorus long before it became fashionable.

This chapter contains a lot of information and exercises to provide you with a broad sampler. I encourage you to experiment with several of the principles to find the ones that make a difference for you. For more in-depth learning, I recommend you consult the resources listed in the reference section at the back of this book.

---

15 Matthieu Ricard www.matthieuricard.com

THE BODY CHECK-IN

Purpose:
To become aware of what is happening with your body, which will help ground you and focus your energy.

Some of you may be quite tuned in to your body and some of you may never have stopped to consider what your body is doing, until you have overtaxed it in some way and are feeling the effects. To get a barometer of how tuned in to your body you are, take a moment to breathe deeply and observe what is happening. How open does your body feel? How is the energy moving? Where you are feeling tension? Could you describe those feelings in detail to someone?

When you are fully aware of your body, you literally open yourself up to a feeling of closeness with all of the people you encounter in the world. Energy follows awareness. It is easy to bring awareness to your body with a very simple technique called a "body check-in" or "body scan." No matter where you are reading this right now, I want you to take a moment and literally "check-in" with yourself. You can do this anywhere, anytime, to bring awareness back to your body, which will ground you and focus your energy. A simple two minutes in the car (while parked!) before you head into a meeting will do wonders for focusing and grounding yourself.

THE BODY CHECK-IN EXERCISE

Close your eyes. (Oh, how can you read this if your eyes are closed?) Okay, read this and then close your eyes and continue. You may want to have a friend read this slowly while you scan your body, or alternatively, record it and play it back.

While you are doing a body check-in, or scan, breathe deeply. Start at the top of your head and work down through your body. Notice where you are holding any tension; feel any discomfort or constriction of your breathing. Breathe deeply. As you exhale, let any constriction leave your body with your breath. Does your scalp feel tight? Massage your temples. Are your eyes tired from perhaps too much computer work? Scrunch them together tightly and then release them. To release any tension in your facial muscles (of which there are 53!), scrunch your entire face together, hold for three seconds and release. If your face and jaw and neck are feeling any tension, massage them and the area around them gently. Move your attention down the body to the shoulder area. Many of us hold the cares of the world in the neck and shoulders. To release the tension, gently move your neck from side to side. Lift your shoulders up to your ears, hold for three seconds and release. Keep checking in as you scan down the body, into your chest area and heart. Inhale deeply. Exhale any tension you are feeling. Feel the sensation of opening up your heart and expanding it and opening your chest cavity. Check-in to your stomach – is it quiet or churning, full or empty? Just notice and breathe; then focus down to the core area, your power center and down your legs to your feet. Unlock your legs, bend your knees slightly and shake out your legs if you are feeling glued to the ground. Feel the power of the earth below your feet and feel the tingle of energy as you receive it from the ground.

Your Body check-in will show you what you are bringing into any situation or conversation, and by focusing on breathing and being mindful of what is happening with your body, you will begin to still your racing mind and refocus yourself to be open and present. Experiment with self-observation in different situations. Notice when your heart begins to race, when your breathing gets shallow or deeper or if you are holding your breath. Feel when your shoulders tense, your jaw clenches. As you notice physical sensations, take your attention back to the breath and breathe through those sensations to release them.

BREATHING BASICS

BREATH AWARENESS

Take a moment to notice your breathing. Watch and feel the movement of the breath, do not attempt to change it in any way. Focus on inhaling through your nostrils and exhaling through your mouth. Focus on breathing deeply right down to your belly area. Find the stillness within (tune in to your inner radio station frequency). Notice where you have any resistance in the body and consciously breathe into that space. Focus on your breath, and then focus again. Opening your physical being opens you up to possibilities.

BREATHING FROM THE CORE

Your physical center is approximately two inches below your navel, deep in your body, between the front of the abdomen and spine. According to Zen Buddhists and Japanese belief, it is in the center (the Hara) where vital forces reside, and it is also from this point where deep breathing must be originated. I refer to this area as your "Core." When you do breathing or grounding exercises, you may want to put your hands on your core area to remind you to breathe deeply into your Core rather than taking shallow breaths that originate in your chest.

> "Your center is your bodily and energetic "base camp" that can be used as a way to focus, learn and move through transitions. It helps you to feel bodily present to yourself and your situation. The state of center is a doorway to begin feeling your possibilities in the world, not as a rigid quality, but as a state to help you develop and access other parts of yourself. You can tap your belly to shift your attention (to center) quickly, bringing you to an openness and greater willingness to see and sense what is happening without the distraction of your automatic ideas and opinions."[16]

---

16 Suzanne Zeman, *Listening to Bodies: A Somatic Primer for Coaches, Managers and Executives* (Shasta Gardens Publishing, 2008) p. 79

Your center is essentially the starting point, the focal point where you can always return. In a sense, your center is like "home," a safe place to anchor yourself and from which to operate.

YOGA NOSTRIL BREATHING

Purpose:
Yoga nostril breathing is a beautiful technique to use if you are nervous, tense, worried, and/or having pre-performance jitters. According to a study in Applied Psychophysiology and Biofeedback, this breathing technique can actually lower your blood pressure.[17] Do this anywhere, anytime, to calm yourself, empty your mind and focus.

Try it:
Hold your right nostril closed and inhale through the left. Close the left nostril and exhale through the right and then inhale through it. Close the right and exhale through the left. Inhale through the left and continue alternating. Focus on the Breathing.

THE NOW EXERCISE[18]

Purpose:
To clear your mind, relax, become present. Breath counting is a Zen practice – it is a deceptively simple technique with meditative benefits.

Try it:
1. Count your breaths from one to ten. As you do this, mentally focus on the numbers and on saying to yourself IN-one, OUT-one; IN-two and OUT-two, IN-three and OUT-three, etc.
2. If you lose count before you get to ten (and pretty much everyone does lose count at first), simply begin again at one.
3. When you get to ten, smile down into your heart.

---

17 *Women's Health Magazine*, June 2009 p. 28
18 The NOW exercise copyright Michael Neill from his book *Feel Happy Now* www.geniuscatalyst.com

FOCUSING: KEEPING THE MAIN THING THE MAIN THING

"The successful man is the average man, focused."

– unknown

One of the biggest things standing in the way of living into our performance potential, either on or off stage, is the challenge of being present and 100% focused on the now. Our swirling world-in-a-New-York-minute lifestyles and our obsession with multi-tasking has created a huge challenge for us to focus on one thing and ever really simply "be". To really achieve a peak performance in anything, however, you absolutely must have laser focus on the task at hand and be completely present. We discussed strategies for reducing mental interferences in more depth in Chapter Two. Being aware and present in the now is critical to maintaining 100% focus. Strategies to empty your mind of the myriad of thoughts crowding in and allowing yourself to be completely present in the now will open up your intuition, creativity and inspiration.

GETTING PRESENT

Purpose:
To empty your mind, become aware and truly be present in the now.

1. While Sitting

Put your hands on your desk or the arms of your chair or somewhere that they are supported. Close your eyes. Focus all of your attention on your hands. You may begin to feel a warmth or tingling sensation in them. Now focus intensely on the inside of your hands, feel the energy moving through your hands, feel the blood coursing through your veins. Soon you feel the palms of your hands begin to tingle. This is the energy working. Continue to focus all of your attention on your hands and the energy being generated. Take a deep breath and open your eyes. You are present.

2. Anywhere, Anytime

Mantras are a technique I use to redirect and open my mind to bring me back to the present anywhere or anytime. Mantras are energy-based tools of power or phrases of energy that can change a state of consciousness.

This is my favorite (Recite and repeat several times): *I AM PRESENT * THIS IS NOW * I AM HERE.*

CENTERING

Purpose:

To become more "present," more mindful and more aware.

> "Center is a state of being that is not confined to certain posture… ultimately, center is an inner subjective state that is manifested through the body. In other words, we can relate to center from any number of positions or actions. Lying down, sitting, carrying a sleeping child, washing the dishes, or driving a car can all be done from center. Being with center is an attitude toward ourself, and this attitude… is one in which we feel bodily present to ourself and our situation. Center is a state where we come into relationship with our bodily self in a way that is balanced and present."[19]

Try it:

At any point in the day when you feel yourself getting overwhelmed, or just plain running around without thinking, take a moment to center yourself, to breathe into your heart, soften it and fill it with love. This "being" with the world will allow all of your action to flow more consistently and be more connected.

CENTERING YOURSELF WHILE STANDING

- Stand with your feet shoulder-width apart and balanced slightly on the balls of your feet.
- Knees should be unlocked but not too bent.
- Your spine is upright, but not rigid. Visualize lengthening your spine from the inside.
- Relax your shoulders. If you feel tension in them hold them up to your ears for three seconds and then release.
- Drop your head onto your chest; feel the weight of it.
- Let the weight of your head take your upper body over, so you flop from the waist.

---

19 Richard Strozzi Heckler, *The Anatomy of Change*, (Berkley: North Atlantic Books 1984) p. 82

- Shake your shoulders out while bent over.
- Check that your knees remained unlocked and the back of your neck is released.
- Curl up slowly from the base of spine.
- Let your shoulders fall easily into place – avoid the temptation to place them.
- The head is the last thing that should come up.
- Keep breathing, jaw should be free.
- Allow yourself to relax into your centeredness.

CENTERING YOURSELF WHILE SITTING

- As you sit, feel how you are holding your body, what is supporting you – where you feel the weight.
- Put your feet flat on the floor and sit upright, hands resting comfortably on your upper thighs. Let them fall to where they naturally drop.
- Lift your shoulders up to your ears and hold them for three seconds, then release them and allow them to relax.
- Breathe deeply into your core area.
- Rock yourself gently from side to side and front to back until you feel a place where you feel most balanced and just relax into it.
- Breathe into your heart and feel the warmth as you imagine a pink light fills and expands it.
- Take your attention down to your core. Continue to breathe from the belly area.
- Take three deep inhalations and exhalations.

GROUNDING

Purpose:
To focus our energy for more power, effectiveness and stability.

In my youth, I don't remember ever understanding what being "grounded" might mean except maybe with some vague reference to electrical terms – having heard when some electrical wiring shorted out that it wasn't grounded. Later on I intellectually understood that those solid, stable, salt-of-the-earth people who I knew, were grounded. Indeed, "grounding," in the sense we are talking about, is the process of connecting ourselves to the earth's energies.

First, observe your posture and your breath. Before starting movement – take your attention to the heart. Open the heart – visualize a pink light filling your heart and softening it.

INDIVIDUAL GROUNDING EXERCISE

- Sit (or stand) comfortably, and then close your eyes.
- Breathe slowly and deeply from the core, counting down from ten to one.
- Continue to breathe deeply as you imagine that you are on the top floor of a tall building and there is a long cord attached to the base of your spine extending down through all the floors and way down into the earth.
- Visualize this cord being like a root grounded deep into the earth, so strongly connected to the earth that it gathers all of the energy of the earth.
- Now imagine the energy of the earth is flowing up through this cord; up through all the floors, then bursting through your floor and up the cord into your spine.
- Feel this spread up your spine and through all of your veins and arteries up to the base of your head, and then into your head until you feel your whole body filled with this energy.
- Feel the flow of the energy go right out the top of your head. Picture this flow of energy until it is well established.

- Now imagine the universe's energy flowing back in through your head, down that long cord down your spine and through your feet into the earth. The two flows are mixing harmoniously. The earth's energy and the energy of the universe are flowing through you.
- Continue to breathe. Open your eyes and smile!

CHORUS GROUNDING EXERCISE
(easily adaptable for any group or team situation)

- Close your eyes. Inhale and exhale deeply: in through your nose, out through your mouth.
- As you do this, imagine with each successive breath that you are drawing in good energy and focusing your mind on the present. Exhale all of the thoughts about the stuff that happened before you got here tonight – your bad day at work, the traffic…
- Exhale all of the stuff you are thinking about that you didn't do today and have to take care of when you get home. For the next three hours, you are here: 100% present.
- Breathe. Take two deep belly breaths.
- Focus on the bottoms of your feet. Take all of your conscious awareness to the bottom of your feet.
- You will begin to feel a tingling. Feel the tingling.
- Visualize yourself walking into a forest, a beautiful forest with sunlight streaming through the trees.
- Pick your own beautiful tall tree.
- Put your arms around it. Feel the strength your tree holds and the energy it contains.
- Bend your knees slightly.
- Feel the energy of the tree merging with your energy, traveling down through your legs and feet and into the earth.
- As the energy descends, your energy is traveling with it, meshing with the tree roots. Your energy is completely connected – connected right to the magma – the fire in the center of the earth. You are completely connected to the core of the earth. Allow it to flow.
- Feel the fire. Feel the warmth begin to spread throughout your body and settle in your belly – the core – your base camp.

- You are completely entwined, protected by and connected to the roots, feeling the fire of the molten rock at the center of the earth.
- Let the energy now ascend.
- Begin to bring the energy up from the roots through the ground – up through the bottom of your feet and into your toes. Feel them and feel your feet tingle. Make them tingle.
- The energy surges upward. Bring that tingle up into your legs, into your bone marrow, into your hips.
- Keep this connection from the core.
- Draw that energy up to the core where the fire of the earth is burning in your belly, your core: your source of personal power, and then to the heart where your emotion is.
- Focus on someone you love deeply. Feel their energy expand your heart.
- Feel the energy flow through your heart.
- Feel your heart bathed in the warmth of love.
- Up through the chest into your arms, hands and fingers, feel the tingle constantly.
- Take the energy up to your throat where your voice is. Feel that energy permeating the tissue of your vocal folds.
- Pass your energy up through your eyes and mind.
- All the while keep the fire burning in your core area.
- Feel yourself connected through to the earth.
- Rising away above your head the energy pours out. Raise your arms above your head. Feel the energy pouring out. Spread your arms to the sides. Feel the energy surround and envelop you and your chorus riser mates. Feel the universe return the energy through the top of your head and course through your body, mingling with the energy coursing up your body from the earth.
- You and your chorus are surrounded by unlimited energy. This powerful ball of unlimited energy is not just you, but your whole chorus. It is your chorus.
- You can access this energy at any time – in seconds. You are ready.
- Open your eyes. You are grounded and energized.

ENERGY

Now that we have gotten our mental and emotional mind-sets in order we are ready to harness the power of our own energetic connection to the universe. I am sure you have experienced the power of energy perhaps when meeting someone else: you are drawn into them with almost a physical pull. You might say they have charisma... or a certain "je ne sais quoi"... (I don't know what)... a certain "something." All you know is that you want it!

Have you ever experienced it for yourself, when you create a feeling of grounded connection with the world and it seems as if everyone is smiling at you as you walk down the street? When you give your energy in a way the world can receive it and then give it back to you, you have created an incredibly powerful vehicle. Once you become aware and grounded and present, you realize you are much more than just your human form or your thoughts, and you begin to understand the potential of the energy within you.

I am sure you have seen and experienced the power of grounded energy (or lack of it) in a performance setting many times. In the world of a cappella chorus competitions, you will have heard choruses sing beautifully, even masterfully, looking great and with inventive choreography, but who are forgettable as soon as they leave the stage. Then there are choruses who blow your mind with their talented singing and dancing and their presence. Their performance seems to grab you from inside and pull you outward until you feel almost as if you are onstage with them. They take your breath away. They capture the mood and the enraptured attention of the whole auditorium and everyone seems to be engulfed in a big tsunami of energy. That is presence. Presence is energy. It is grounded energy that makes the difference. Grounded energy is very powerful. It can make every person in an auditorium sit on the edge of their seats barely breathing and so quiet that a pin could drop as they wait for the next note to be sung. It can make thousands of people jump to their feet simultaneously as the final chord is rung.

We can develop an awesome amount of energy when needed and it requires very little effort or time. All things arise from thought. Think of filling your being with energy. Your body is a perfect piece of equipment under your mind's control. When you use this energy combined with your mind-set and skills, the world of possibility bursts wide open.

CREATING YOUR ENERGY BALL[20]

Purpose:
To feel energy and expand it; getting in touch with your personal energy is the first step. (Remember our favorite word… awareness?)

- Sit or stand with your eyes closed, feet planted, knees slightly bent.
- Ground yourself, and when you feel fully connected to the earth, begin rubbing the palms of your hands together briskly, remembering to breathe deeply from your core. At the center of each of our palms, we all have a very high-energy point. Rubbing our palms together stimulates the growth of this energy.
- Within a short time, you will feel a slight tingling or warmth between your palms. This is the energy building.
- Stop rubbing your hands and cup them as if holding a softball.
- Concentrate on the feeling between your hands while you continue to breathe deeply.
- Start moving your hands in and out slightly and see if you can feel a slight resistance or sponginess between them. This is your energy ball. As you practice, you will find that you feel this resistance more and more strongly, even as you move your hands farther apart.
- See how large you can make your "energy ball." This is the energy of your own body, which is always available to you.
- Move your hands to your core, returning the energy to your body to revitalize and energize it.
- Open your eyes and feel exhilarated and full of power.

BODY POWER TECHNIQUE

Purpose:
To stimulate your individual personal energy.

- Place your hands just below the navel at the core, your power center, your energy center.
- Close your eyes.

---

20 Energy-ball and body-power concepts are courtesy of Vi Feist.

- Visualize your core area, your energy center. Put your attention there. Feel the power and strength within that core area.
- Visualize a 1000-watt light bulb in your body, in your core. It is glowing and getting brighter. The warmth is filling your core area, and the energy is burning brightly. It is pumping energy and stamina through your body. Breathe from the core, the gut.
- Envision that light bulb: glowing, glowing. See the energy field around it getting brighter and brighter, spreading from your core throughout your body.
- As you continue to visualize this, the energy in your body is stimulated.
- Open your eyes.

Purpose:
To stimulate the energy for a group situation.

- Place your hands just below the navel at the core, your power center, your energy center.
- Close your eyes.
- Visualize your core area, your energy center. Put your attention there. Feel the power and strength within that core area.
- Visualize a 1000-watt light bulb in your body, in your core. It is glowing and getting brighter, the warmth is filling your core area, and the energy is burning bright and is pumping energy and stamina through your body. Breathe from the core, the gut.
- Envision that light bulb: glowing, glowing. See the energy field around it getting brighter and brighter, spreading from your core throughout your body.
- As you continue to visualize this, the energy in your body is stimulated.
- Continue taking the light inside you, the burning energy, and expanding it. Take it outside your body and expand it to the people standing beside you and in front of and behind you. Continue to expand your light to encompass the entire auditorium. The whole auditorium is bathed in and glowing with a bright ball of energy with you in the center of it. You are connected through your energy with the entire auditorium.
- Open your eyes.

THREE DIMENSIONAL ENERGY

I first heard about the concept of three-dimensional energy from Master Somatic Coach, Suzanne Zeman,[21] who works from the body with coaches, executives and business teams to develop their presence, awareness and vision.

Purpose:
To add and connect with all three energy dimensions (length, width, depth). This will greatly enhance your grounded presence and effective being in the world. Just as in singing, where we want to access three dimensional vocal resonance and use three dimensional breathing, we can further enhance our performance possibilities in any area of our lives by accessing all three dimensions of energy.

Try it:
1. We already have had some time to practice accessing our *length* or vertical energy dimension by centering ourselves, grounding ourselves and connecting with the incredible energy of the earth. We feel almost as though our spine has lengthened from the inside and we can easily tap into the core of the earth to bring energy up into our body and outward to connect to others. The length energy dimension has grounded us.

2. The energy dimension of *width* is the embracing "social dimension."[22] As you expand your energy out to your sides, you naturally begin to include those people around you. This is a fabulous energy dimension to use to help connect with others. Consider adding this width dimension of energy whenever you need to connect to groups of people – if you are leading a workshop or a meeting, or perhaps going to a party you are nervous about. This is an extremely critical energy dimension to access in a chorus situation so there is a unified feeling with all of the chorus members.

   To help access this width dimension, first make sure you are grounded and connected to the earth through your length energy dimension. As you bring the energy up your body, simply expand your arms from

---

21 Learn more about Suzanne Zeman's work at www.somaticbusinesscoach.com
22 Suzanne Zeman, *Listening to Bodies: A Somatic Primer for Coaches, Managers and Executives* (Shasta Gardens Publishing, 2008) p. 81

your sides and feel the energy extend outwards, filling in the space between your body and your arms. Get the feeling that you are physically opening yourself and expanding your energy to include others. Be sure to stay grounded with the length dimension of energy as you add the width dimension.

3. The dimension of *depth* extends behind you and in front of you. This energy dimension can provide support behind you as well as move you forward. To develop the depth dimension, make sure you are connected length-wise to the core of the earth and bring the energy up your body. As you do, put one hand on your lower back and gradually extend your hand behind you: breathe into that space. Once you feel that energy fill the space behind you to back you up, use your other hand to expand the energy forward to embrace your dreams and goals.

CHANGING ENERGY LEVELS

There are three types of energy we can choose to manifest at any time. We use a combination of all three types to varying degrees as we go through our daily lives. Our ideal is choosing to use "connected energy" as often as possible – this kind of energy ensures you are really present in the world.

1. Withheld Energy

Most of the people in this world go through their days keeping their energy close inside to varying degrees. You sense this especially in a big city, as on public transit where everyone is dutifully protecting his or her personal space. No one is sharing his or her energy. What happens when someone gets on the bus over the top with energy? Those on the bus look away. They do not engage. There is no energy exchange. Withheld energy is not expressed outwardly. Many times we are simply preoccupied, thus withhold our energy. This is introspective energy. Your energy barely extends past the boundaries of your physical body. If you are in learning or thinking mode, you are usually withholding energy. You can feel it when you walk into a room of people – some people feel closed and some you are drawn into because they are connecting and exchanging energy.

2. Imposed Energy

The polar opposite to "withholding energy" is "imposed energy." Imposed energy is ultra exuberant, extreme, almost manic and ultimately alienating. It doesn't feel authentic when received. It does not seek to connect to individuals. Usually it exists to try to "make" something happen in a situation. It is not energy that is exchanged; it is energy that is imposed. An example of "imposed" energy would be the super salesperson desperately trying to sell you a product you do not want, or perhaps a leader who is trying to get you motivated by aggressively whipping you into a frenzy.

Imposed energy is useful energy when you want to: get your family out of house so they aren't late for school, organize a fire drill, or give instructions to a crowd to organize the line-up at the buffet table. Imposed energy is not an energy that seeks to connect with others.

3. Connected Energy

The third kind of energy is "connected energy" – your energy is going out, but it is also coming back to you. Connected energy is about being present with the world, and its people. It is energy that you might feel, for instance, if you walk down the street looking at people and smiling. Most people will smile back at you and suddenly everyone seems happier. Your energy is connecting with them and they are giving energy back to you. It is a feeling of awareness and of being 100% here, right now. You seem to be at one with the universe.

Think of the times this "connection" has happened for you, about the most profound moments of connection you have ever felt with someone. Perhaps it was a romantic love, or the complete connection you felt while looking into your baby's eyes, or when you felt so connected with a performer or an audience that it was as though you were sharing their energy field.

This grounded and connected energy is called "presence." Connecting your energy is the most powerful way to be really in this world during your day-to-day life or while onstage. It takes focus and openness to connect your energy, but you will find it to be a most profound communication connection.

INDIVIDUAL EXERCISE – Changing Energy Levels

Experiment with your three kinds of energy:

1. Walk down the street and "withhold" – what happens?

2. Walk down the street and consciously "connect" with the world, feel as one with the universe.

3. Get into an elevator and "impose" your energy on the people in the elevator. Be over-the-top energetic and perky and notice the reaction of the people around you.

CHORUS GROUP EXERCISE – Changing Energy Levels

Purpose:
To give the chorus and director a strong sense of how the different kinds of energy affect their performance. When we perform, we want to have complete grounded connected energy – we need to "be with" our audience.

Withheld Energy:
Do a run-through of a portion of a song asking the chorus to "withhold" their energy. For some, that may be a difficult task, as their default is to give it all. For those, a technique such as asking them to think of their shopping list, or think about the things they need to do at work the next day, will have the same effect – anything that preoccupies their minds, and takes them away from being truly present in that moment. Make sure the chorus is still performing; they are simply not focusing on performing. The effect of being on autopilot will cause them to withhold energy.

Debrief with the chorus and ask how that felt. Let them know how it felt for you in the audience.

Imposed Energy:
Sing the same portion again, this time giving the chorus the instruction that you want them to be "as hyper as possible, with as much over-the-top energy as they can give." Have them think about when they have been really excited, as if they have just won a competition, and now they have to sing for an audience, when all they really want to do at that moment is scream and jump up and down. Ask them to "Make sure the audience knows how excited you are."

Debrief with the chorus and ask how "imposed energy" felt. Let them know what you felt in the audience.

Connected Energy:
Finally, sing the same portion of the song again, asking the chorus to completely "connect" their energy to the audience. Their goal as a performer is to have the entire audience feel so connected to them that they are swarmed for their autograph as they enter the lobby after their performance.

Ground them, bring their energy up, and ask them to visualize a specific person in the audience to connect to and exchange energy with as they sing. Ask them think consciously of joining energy fields with the director, and through her, expanding their energy field to connect with the audience.

Debrief with the chorus and ask how that felt. Let them know what you felt in the audience.

6

BRAIN GAIN
Utilizing the Power of the Mind

"With the power of soul, anything is possible.
With the power of you, anything you wanna do."

– Jimi Hendrix, from the song, *"Power of Soul"*

I was first introduced to the concept of "affirmations" back in the early 1990s when a friend gave me a deck of new age self-help cards. They were affirmation cards developed by author and speaker, Louise Hay.[23] On the front of each card was a different statement such as "I am flexible and flowing" or "My thoughts are creative." On the back of the card was an affirmation giving more detail and substance to that affirmation. Although there were no directives on how best to use these cards, I began by picking a card from the deck each day, putting it in my wallet, reading it frequently and using that as my affirmation for the day. I used these affirmation cards like an inspirational quote, or a mantra, that I would look at and read out during the day. The cards provided a way to put my mind in a positive place. Although blindly choosing a card from a deck seemed rather random – the concept was sound. I didn't know how affirmations worked back then, I just knew they made me feel good and gave me a feeling that somehow I was in control of my world.

---

23 Louise Hay, author and founder of Hay House, Inc., the international leader in inspirational and self-help publishing. www.louisehay.com

Since my flirtation twenty years ago with the impact of my mind's subconscious workings through the use of affirmation cards, the common knowledge and understanding about how the brain works has developed considerably. There is an acceptance of and movement toward learning more about how we can use the power of our minds to create and influence our world.

The brain consists of millions of cells called neurons. Thoughts and actions form connections and neural pathways through this massive network of cells. New thoughts or activities open up new routes through this network and constantly repeated actions follow the same routes. Each time the same thought or action occurs, that particular neural path takes on a stronger imprint.

Rapidly catching on as positive self-management tools, more and more people are using the techniques of Affirmations and Creative Visualization to achieve astounding results in their lives. They are two enormously effective mental training techniques or tools that are simple to integrate into any part of your life for immediate positive effect.

AFFIRMATIONS

"Whatever the mind can conceive and believe, it can achieve."

– Napoleon Hill, author

WHAT IS AN AFFIRMATION?

An affirmation is an announcement in present tense of some condition you want to create in the future. Affirmations are really statements of a goal or a desired outcome already in its concluded state. Affirmations are effective ways of using the power of positive thinking to bring you to a state of mind, or to a conclusion you really want.

Stemming from where you put your focus (see Chapter One) and the principle of putting your focus on what you want in the future to open up the possibilities in your life, what you affirm impacts the subconscious mind and silently works to affect your behavior and actions in a positive way. It is believed that using affirmation techniques consistently for thirty days will create a neural shift and your brain will reprogram itself at a subconscious level.

HOW TO CREATE AN AFFIRMATION

1. Affirm a state or result that you want

Start with the words "I Am" or "We Are." e.g., going for a job interview about which you are really nervous, you might create a simple affirmation like "I am calm and confident and fully prepared."

Lions Gate Chorus used an affirmation before their successful 3rd place International Competition performance to affirm the state that they most wanted to reinforce as a group in order to achieve their peak performance. Key words in this affirmation were: "grounded" and "confident"; and the words "passion" and "total abandon" were cues to inspire the understated Canadians to really let themselves go.

"We are grounded and confident. We are singing and performing at an "A" level of excellence with artistry, passion and total abandon."

– Lions Gate Chorus affirmation

2. Use the present tense

As you write your affirmation, consider that it has already happened or that you already have it. When you state something to yourself as if it were true today, your behavior will come into alignment with the belief.

Let's say you are looking for a relationship. You will get a more positive effect for an affirmation like "I have a wonderful fulfilling relationship with a man I am passionate about," as opposed to "I will find a relationship with someone I can be passionate about someday."

3. State in the positive

Whatever we focus our energy on magnifies. Choose a positive focus. For example: "I am happy and joyful and enjoying my fun-filled life" is much stronger than "I don't want to be unhappy and bored in my life anymore."

4. Affirm what you want, not what you don't want

As we discussed in Chapter One, keeping your focus on the positive side creates possibilities. The universe has a very hard time responding to a negative request.

5. Make your intent clear

Be crystal clear and specific about what it is you are affirming.

HOW TO MAKE YOUR AFFIRMATIONS EVEN MORE EFFECTIVE

1. Write them out and keep them handy

Write out your affirmation several times. If you are a visual person you might want to draw pictures around your affirmation. Post your affirmations where you can see them daily. Keep your affirmation with you – in your wallet, on your car dashboard, on your mirror at home, on your screen saver.

For instance, as I write this book I am staring at my affirmation taped to my computer. *"I am an inspired writer. My words are flowing and my creativity is boundless."*

2. Use your affirmations daily

We talk to ourselves constantly throughout the day. Make part of that self-talk your affirmation. Say it frequently (at least three times per day or more). Say your affirmation before you fall asleep at night, and program your subconscious mind as you drift off into dreamland. Say your affirmation first thing in the morning, before you even get out of bed. Set up your day with a positive intention. Say your affirmation as a re-focusing technique any time as you go through your day.

> My quartet, Fandango, always has an incredibly busy public performance schedule at Christmas time. We frequently have two or three outdoor gigs in one day and in often less than optimum singing conditions – snow, rain, with traffic noise, etc. – it can be easy to forget why we are doing it. In order to focus our minds on our reasons for doing our public performances, we huddle together at the beginning of the day and, with fervor and enthusiasm, recite our affirmation. If we need to ground ourselves between gigs, we recite it again.

> *"We are grounded and confident and singing with a rich resonant sound. We are having fun as we spread the love and joy of Christmas wherever we go."*

> – Fandango Quartet affirmation

3. Amplify your affirmation with feeling

When you say your affirmations, evoke as much feeling as you can. This is like injecting your affirmation with rocket fuel!

> Lions Gate Chorus recited their affirmation at the beginning of every rehearsal leading up to the international singing competition in order to set the framework of possibility for the rehearsal hall. They created a powerful unit feel by putting their hands on the shoulders of the women in front of them as they recited it. The impact of 120 women passionately reciting their group affirmation in unison, making each word important, was a very powerful and unifying energy boost.

4. Use affirmations wildly

Create as many affirmations as you want for any part of your life. Use affirmations for a personal reason, use them for business success and try them out in a group or team situation. Clarifying intent and as a group reciting what you want before, say, a group project, will add a cohesive focus and energy to propel the entire team forward faster. Any situation will benefit from the use of affirmations. (e.g., if you are stuck in a huge traffic jam: "I am calm, cool and collected. I know that I will get to my destination on time. I am thankful for having a car to drive.")

Julie T. relates the story about how she started using affirmations to get over her fear of public speaking – a change necessitated by a new job that required her to speak in public. "I accepted a new job position as a trainer, facilitator, and a bit of a mentor and manager, which was a huge leap in responsibility for me. I was scared and anticipatory, full of apprehension, and self-criticism. Could I do the job? Was I good enough? Could I speak in front of 20, 30, 40 or more people? Did I really, truly have the right stuff? Using affirmations had really worked for me at chorus to develop my belief in myself and personal singing confidence so I thought it couldn't hurt to try it as I embraced my new job, and hey, it was just as effective! When I wrote and recited an affirmation for work, it gave me the confidence necessary to go the whole nine yards. I even spoke in front of 50 people without hesitation!! Wow! Using the affirmation technique in my life has helped me become a better singer, manager, colleague, parent and partner.

"I am grounded and confident. I have done thorough research and understand the content of my material and know that I am a poised, articulate and interesting facilitator."

– Julie's work affirmation

VISUALIZATION

WHAT IS VISUALIZATION?

We have an awesome power within that, for most of us, is largely untapped. Visualization, or creative visualization as it is sometimes referred to, is the use of mental imagery and intention to obtain an objective. A vivid mental picture of the desired thing is created and held firmly fixed in the mind as if it had already happened. Visualization is simply powerfully focused thought in pictures, and it causes equally powerful feelings. Visualizations have been used for years by people in all walks of life to train their minds by creating images in one's mind that support one's goals. Although the technique has been most publicized in its use by professional athletes, visualization techniques can be applied to almost every aspect of human endeavor with great results. Visualization dramatically improves your chances of achieving whatever it is you want to achieve. Research is finding that both physical and psychological reactions in certain situations can be improved with visualization. Guided imagery, visualization, mental rehearsal or other such techniques can maximize the efficiency and effectiveness of your training. In a world where high-level competitions are won by points, or 100th's of seconds, most high-achieving performers will use every possible training technique at hand. Visualization is one way to gain that very slim margin.

HOW TO CREATE A VISUALIZATION

You can visualize virtually anywhere, but a quiet place where you will not be disturbed is best. Simply focus your mind on what you want to do, and keep replaying the internal film of yourself actually doing it. The amazing thing is that it has been proven that the benefit of visualizing the events is actually the same as if you had actually done it.

In effect, visualization is a kind of structured daydream. Unlike daydreaming however, it is done in the first person and in the present tense. You imagine what you would like in a situation and paint a picture in your mind that is as specific as possible and then add sensory images into that picture for even more effect.

After deciding on a goal and coming up with a plan, you need to hold in your mind a clear mental image of your goal. You need to see it accomplished. This step requires that you use your imagination and call up what you want. Sometimes looking at photos of what you want to achieve, and then closing your eyes and trying to see it in your imagination, will enhance your ability to visualize. You also need to focus on your visualization often to give it positive energy.

VISUALIZATIONS FOR PEAK PERFORMANCE

Peak performers in any field can use visualizations to accelerate the achievement of goals. By visualizing in your mind whatever it is you want to achieve and with consistent mental rehearsal, minds and bodies become trained to actually perform the skill imagined.

For example: an Olympic swimmer would visualize himself winning his race, he would view his success in his mind, and he would experience in minute detail every aspect of the race, from a perfect start, to every dive, glide, stroke and flip, to a perfectly timed finish, to the medal ceremony and the raising of his country's flag. By the time he gets to the real race, he has already won it several times; in his mind he already has executed successfully every aspect of his race perfectly. The pattern of success is firmly imprinted in his mind. When the start gun fires, everything will run to his internal script automatically. This gives a powerful advantage over the other competitors.

In a barbershop singing competition, the same principle applies. The participants visualize the goal they want to achieve. A visualization is created and the chorus or quartet is led through that visualization on a consistent basis in the preparation for competition. Both the pre-competition and the performance itself are visualized in vivid detail. By imagining the complete scene visually (seeing pictures), kinesthetically (how your body feels when you are onstage singing), and auditorily (what you hear: the music and the roar of the crowd), the singer can use her mind to call up these images over and over; that ultimately has the same effect as rehearsing a technical skill repeatedly.

The singers can use these techniques to "intend" an outcome of a performance or competition, or simply to create the ultimate performance experience they want. By visualizing a scene, complete with images of a previous best performance or a future desired outcome, the singer is instructed to simply "step into" that feeling. Ultimately, the singer gains complete confidence and complete control over their successful performance and a belief in this new "self" they have visualized.

Leading up to the International Chorus Competition, Betsy used visualization to successfully prepare herself for the stage. She visualized the entire day – from her pre-competition breakfast, to applying her make up, putting on her sparkly red outfit, getting into the backstage traffic pattern and, finally, every moment of performing the competition package on stage.

Betsy then found great benefits in transferring the visualization technique to the tennis court. "Before a tennis match, I'll take the time to visualize – I see the court, see my awesome serve – the toss, the swing, and see myself making those great plays. When I visualize, I bring in everything I can: the look and feel of the outfit I am wearing, the sound of the ball hitting the racquet and how the shot looks on the court. My visualization also includes thinking through how I will remain positive and not let my opponent see my frustration. Visualization helps me focus by both clearing my mind and giving me a sense of calm."

VISUALIZATIONS FOR YOUR LIFE

All you really need to do to visualize anything you want in your life, is to close your eyes and daydream. Dream about your goal as being something you already have. Put that idle daydream into the first person (yes, it is you in the picture) and the present tense (yes, it is happening now, you are there, you are living that dream).

Much like affirmations, you need to make your visualization as specific as possible, with as much detail using all of your senses as possible. Add your positive emotions around that visualization. Add passion.

Most importantly, you need to take action. When you can visualize the path to what you want, you must, of course, be prepared to actually walk it in the real world. If you are a hermit living in a cave, no amount of creative visualization will suddenly bring you a mansion on the ocean with a fabulous social life. You need to take action if you want to make that visualization real.

> Daryl had used visualizations as a technique to get to sleep for several years. The visual she chose was a clear picture of mountains rising over the ocean. The visualization cleared the junk out of her mind, allowing her to drift off to sleep easily. Several years later, Daryl was living in an apartment with a peek-a-boo view of the mountains through the limbs of a large, dead tree. One morning she opened her drapes and the tree had been cut down. In front of her was an unobstructed view of the mountains rising over the ocean, the *identical* picture she had been visualizing to get to sleep for several years!
>
> This was a turning point in her life and reinforced her belief in her dream of living by the water. Daryl took her visualization one step further, and added in the prominent sound of seagulls, and the very powerful smell of the salty air. She believed that one day she would be living peacefully by the ocean. Not long after, by chance, an apartment listing by the beach popped into Daryl's in-box. She saw the apartment and rented it on the spot.
>
> This was her dream. Her visualization had manifested.

EXERCISE: CREATING YOUR OWN VISUALIZATION

What is the result you want to achieve? (e.g., acing your interview, achieving your peak performance, etc.)

Call on your five senses to paint a picture of the result – just as if you are there.

Sight (visual)

Feel (kinesthetic)

Sound (auditory)

Smell (olfactory)

Taste (gustatory)

Find a place where you can relax, time to relax, then close your eyes and live into your visualization.

CHORUS VISUALIZATIONS

The following was a pre-competition performance visualization used by several competing choruses leading up to the 2008 International Chorus competition in Hawaii. In a rehearsal situation, the chorus director led the visualization and then moved directly into the singing of the performance package. It is important to adapt your visualization to create a desired reality for your chorus and to use the touchstone words that will have meaning for your chorus. You may choose to add in specifics for each voice part in the weeks leading up to the competition, especially if you go through the entire singing portion of the visualization. That way, you can affirm the results you want for particular areas. e.g., if you want to reinforce a certain sound quality add that into the affirmation, "We are singing with a rich, resonant sound" – or, for a particular section, "The leads have taken charge and are in complete command of the stage" – , etc. The key is to make it real for *your* situation and chorus needs.

Sample chorus competition visualization:
(Pre-Hawaii Chorus Competition)

Please close your eyes.

You are in Hawaii… and have spent an amazing week in the warm sun-shine, with the friendly Hawaiian people, with your chorus mates and sweet Adeline sisters from around the world. Everywhere you have gone you have felt warmth and positivity. The whole atmosphere has ignited you and you are thrilled and proud to be part of this wonderful organization.

You have spent the time in the Convention center cheering on your quartets, and have closed your eyes and visualized being onstage. You have taken the time to walk to the front of the arena and turn and look back, to the thousands of people in the audience who will be ignited by you while you are onstage. You are ready to rock the world.

The excitement has been building in you for months around this contest: excitement, but deep inside a real sense of calm, of confidence, of certainty. You are prepared. You are ready. You know what you are here to do, and you can't wait to do it.

Each time you have come together with your chorus to rehearse over the course of the week, you have felt stronger, more connected. You can feel the unlimited power and energy of your chorus. There is a big warm feeling in your heart, and it feels like it is almost spilling out of you.

Finally it's Contest morning. You visualized your peak performance from the very beginning note to the roar of the crowd at the final chord before falling asleep the night before and you feel amazingly refreshed and rested when you wake up. The excitement you felt all week has changed to a solid sense of feeling calm and grounded. You feel completely confident and ready to go.

Your chorus time together this day is focused, and your riser mates are calm. You keep your voice warmed up, and makeup and hair all go smoothly today. There are no problems. You get down to the lobby early... ready to get on the bus.

You walk through the backstage traffic pattern... and finally onto the stage. You can already hear the crowd beginning to chant. You are ready to perform. You are completely aware of everything. All of your senses are heightened and you feel a profound sense of being present... being completely present. You are focused on (your director) like a laser – spreading your energy around you to surround your chorus mates, and envelop (your director) and outward over the judges' pit, into the audience. The energy is electric. You are calm and confident. You are ready. Open your eyes.

(Your director) nods to the judges to indicate that you are ready and then beckons for the pitch.

Announcer's voice: "We are ready for the next contestant. Would everyone please be seated. Contestant #_____ representing Region _____. Under the direction of _____, the _____ Chorus."

CUSTOMIZING YOUR GROUP VISUALIZATION EXERCISE

Adapt your visualization for your own unique situation. For your visualization to have the most impact, bring in the five senses as much as possible and use the words that are most meaningful to you and your group.

7

RIGHT HERE, RIGHT NOW
The Power of Intention

"live with intention. walk to the edge. listen hard. practice wellness.
play with abandon. laugh. choose with no regret. appreciate your friends.
continue to learn. do what you love. live as if this is all there is."

– mary anne radmacher[24]

BEING PRESENT

Most of us wind through our days working and playing without a lot of conscious thought about what we are doing at each moment. Our minds are so overtaxed with stimuli and things to do that multi-tasking has now become a survival technique.

We often are no longer present consciously in a current task. Instead, we are off in our heads either into the future or back into the past. It is not uncommon to live whole stretches of time in either the past or the future. One of author Louise Hay's oft-quoted themes is that "the point of power is always in the present moment." We only truly live life when we are present in the moment. To be actually here, in this moment, is incredibly powerful. Being present means being fully conscious and aware of the "now" and using all of our senses to feel what is going on in the now. We feel being present almost as a heightened sense of reality with all of the pictures crisp and in focus.

---

24 Used with permission – mary anne radmacher, *Live With Intention*, Conari Press, 2010.

I had the amazing experience of being present with total aware-ness when I was on stage with Lions Gate Chorus at the 2007 International Chorus Semi-finals Competition. It was as if every-thing was heightened and I was hyper aware of the sounds and the sights around me. Even though the noise from the audience of 7,000 was deafening, I felt I could hear every word each person in the crowd was saying through the cacophony. I could actually vividly even see the dust particles in the beams of light hitting the stage. I was totally aware of each and every note I sang in those six minutes on stage. It was an incredibly profound sensation – to be completely aware and present in the midst of such an awesome event.

If you can remember a time when you were completely present, you will know how powerful that moment can be. It could be something very simple; perhaps sitting outside in nature looking at a bug on a leaf when the noises of nature suddenly become amplified, the colors become more vivid, and you are even aware of your own breath.

Julie S. described the experience of being completely present on stage in an International Quartet Competition finals performance as feeling almost "out-of-body." "When we were singing as one, and the music was so powerful, I was completely out of any thought process, however, I was still acutely aware of the rise and fall of my quartet mate's breath beside me, the stillness of the audience, the color of the atmosphere around us and the feeling of effortlessness and flow within my body."

In any pursuit, being present allows the space for the most inspiration and grounded energy, presence and creative flow.

BEING, NOT DOING

"Be the change you want to see in the world."

– Mahatma Ghandi

There is another option to the filling of our lives with endless "To Do" lists when we find that obsession with the list is actually working contrary to the energy of the universe. By focusing on being, rather than doing, we can become more aware, and begin to harness the incredible energy of the present.

> I once worked with a very "doing-oriented" chorus musical director. She always had a very detailed rehearsal plan, and carefully outlined what needed to be done in each rehearsal for it to be a success. A masterful planner and scheduler, she had developed and was implementing a chorus plan to achieve their goals according to the timeline developed: all very sensible planning!
>
> The problems arose when the director realized that the things on her list were not things she could make happen by sheer force of will. They weren't things that hard work and persistence or even methodical planning could bring about in the chorus by simply putting them on a list and implementing them.
>
> For instance: getting a more emotional delivery from the chorus as they were singing the ballad was not exactly a linear item she could cross off her To Do list and make happen. It became clear through our coaching process together that she was still trying to do it herself. She had not considered that by simply "being" and calling on the resources and collective energy of the chorus to do, that she could allow the power of the universe to help the process in any way.
>
> By trying to get the chorus to do, she was not attracting in the chorus what she wanted, but if she could just "be," the chorus could then connect with her energy and respond. What a relief she felt knowing that she was not the only one with the answer and that she could let go to others to do the work just by trusting them and putting out that energy.

You could see the difference in her. No longer was she fretting about how she was going to get the chorus to do something and trying to make it happen. Instead, just by "being" what she wanted, it actually happened. Her way of being was attracting her success, not what she was doing. She attracted what she wanted not by doing, but by putting herself into vibrational resonance with her desire.

The process of "Just Being" takes a fair degree of guts and trust, but the rewards and impact will be seen almost immediately whenever you can clear your head of Interferences (see Chapter Two) and Limiting Beliefs (Chapter Three) and just be present and get out of the way of the Universe doing its work.

Master Director, Ryan Heller, describes how being "present" changed him. "The mantra *Just Be It*' was one of your coaching highlights that will forever serve to make me a better musician, director and human being. The relief at letting go of the control over the outcome unlocked a world of possibility for me and the chorus."

PAYING ATTENTION

> *A person asked Buddha:*
> *"Are you a God?"*
> *Buddha's reply was*
> *"No."*
> *"Are you an Angel?"*
> *"No."*
> *"Then what are you?"*
> *"I am Awake."*
>
> – Unknown Source

In order to "be," we need to first pay attention. What is going on right now – here – today? What are we feeling? What are we thinking? We need to get in touch with our intuition and to the messages and wisdom we are receiving continuously. We need to stop and listen and trust the messages we hear. We need to be present, staying here in the moment and listening to and trusting our gut. When we do, all sorts of unexpected things begin to happen.

How to start paying Attention:

1. Stop – Yes, I mean that. Just stop. Whether it is for five minutes or a full day, give yourself the gift of stopping. Stop multi-tasking. Stop the schedule and the pressured time grid. Stop the running around. Pull your car over to the side of the road. Close your office door. Close your eyes. Breathe.

2. Center yourself – In a centered state your mind is quiet, and you are open, self-aware and connected with the universe. Take your attention to your breathing, and focus on the feel of the air going in and out.

"Meditation is not a way of making your mind quiet. It is a way of entering into the quiet that is already there – buried under the 50,000 thoughts the average person thinks every day."

– Deepak Chopra[25]

3. Listen – When you have entered the quiet underneath your conscious thought, listen. Listen to what your body is saying, your mind, your heart and your gut. Become aware of the energy within you and around you. Listen to your intuition; listen to the sounds around you. Just notice, be aware. Just be.

4. Act – When you act, consider acting with intention.

---

25 Deepak Chopra, www.deepakchopra.com

BEING INTENTIONAL

"Every intention sets energy into motion
whether you are conscious of it or not."

– Gary Zukav[26]

Considering and then adding an *intention* to an action creates a different level of consciousness and consequent energy around the action. Creating and using intentions focuses your mind on one thing, and in doing so, clears all of the other noise that gets in the way.

For example, I can go through my days marking things off my To Do list or I can pick an item and deliberately consider an intention behind that item. Let's say I have "workout" on my list for today. I can sandwich the gym as a To Do task between my two afternoon appointments, rush there and sweat, and then rush off to the next appointment, or I can hold "workout" as a single task and choose an intention for it that I carry with me during my workout: "Today I am going to be aware of giving my body the best workout possible and notice how fabulous the workings of my body are." Consciously I have shifted and made that workout more powerful simply by holding a specific intention for it.

You can use the Power of Intention for a small action, or a big one. You can even think about this concept in the morning and create an intention for an entire day. Anyone who is leading a group has the potential to make a huge impact by using this simple technique. I use this very important principle of the Power of Intention extensively with directors as they lead rehearsals. By thinking of a singular intention before beginning rehearsal, a leader can effectively create a powerful and focused energy connection that opens an atmosphere of amazing possibility. For example, let's say your chorus is particularly nervous or lacks confidence about an upcoming performance. You might think of holding as your intention for rehearsal that night something as simple as "I am going to chorus tonight to instill confidence." Hold that intention for yourself throughout the evening as you go about your regular manner of directing. Don't specifically modify your technique; just hold the intention in your mind.

You will find that, without consciously changing your directing style or format one iota, you unconsciously will shift how you are showing up and

---

26 Gary Zukav, *Seat of the Soul* (N.Y.: Simon & Schuster, Inc., 1989) p. 123

the energy and mood of the chorus will shift automatically. The intention you have created becomes the foundation for all of the work that you will do that evening.

> Master Director, Sandy Marron, started thinking about The Power of Intention during her four-hour commute to her Lions Gate Chorus rehearsals back in August of 2007. Rehearsals were at a stall and I had recently started coaching Sandy on the "inner coaching" principles.
>
> One of the first things Sandy embraced was the concept of The Power of Intention. By creating and holding a singular intention for each rehearsal, she was able to clear her head of interference and be totally present.
>
> Sandy said, "The first time I created an intention for rehearsal, it went something like this: Tonight at rehearsal, I am going to create an environment where my singers feel like they can accomplish anything, without any boundaries."
>
> "When I held that intention in my mind, I didn't actually consciously do anything differently, but the effect on the chorus was that they were more relaxed, but at the same time, worked harder than ever. They laughed hard, they worked hard, they sang easily. It was an "A" level night, in every way."

USING THE POWER OF INTENTION

Using Intention in the Workplace

Try this one at the workplace one day if you have been experiencing some tense or stressful times at work. "Today I am going to work to spread joy." Write your intention out, put it in your wallet, and say it aloud ten times. Refer back to it during the day. It doesn't matter what the specific activities of your day are. You will be approaching them with a different underlying intention. It is incredible how that one simple thing focuses your energy and makes things shift.

Experiment with intention in a staff meeting that you are leading: e.g., your intention for the staff meeting might be "I want to make all of my team feel respected and valued." How will you show up at the meeting when that is your underlying intention?

Using Intention in Challenging Conversations

Experiment with intention when you have that age-old conversation with your teenager about forgetting to call when they were going to be late coming home from the party. What if your intention is to make sure your teen knows how much you love and respect him or her? You don't need to think about changing what you are going to say. Your words and your tone automatically will change if you change your intention. Imagine how differently your teen might hear: "Johnny I need you to call me if you are going to be late" if your intention for the conversation is to show how much you love and respect him.

Using intention: chorus performance exercise

Have half the chorus come off the risers and face the other half as their audience.

Give the chorus members who are still on the risers a singular intention for singing a specific song.

For example, if your contest ballad is "My Buddy" you might give them the following intention – "Your sole intention for singing this song is to make the audience feel how much you love your Buddy." That is your sole intention, the only thing that you need to have running through your mind – how much you love your Buddy. Have the audience simply be an audience (as opposed to your fellow chorus mates who know every nuance in the song). After the group on the risers sings it through, have the group on the floor tell them how they felt.

It is amazing how a singular intention clarifies and creates a laser focus for the energy and message of the song to come through for the audience. The singers will find that having a singular intention is completely freeing and they are be able to access parts of themselves they had forgotten were there.

This is an especially effective exercise for perhaps a song that you have had a very technical approach to, where people are still very much in their left-brain while singing – or in an uptune with choreography that is distracting the chorus. Once they are given a singular intention on which to focus, it frees up space for the creative, for possibility.

8

COACHING
The Language of Possibility

"You cannot teach a person anything;
you can only help him find it within himself."

– Galileo Gallilei

B ack in the 1500s, Galileo hit on what is the fundamental core belief of the coaching movement – that each one of us knows what is best for ourselves. At the heart of coaching is the assumption that every individual is whole, creative and resourceful and not only has the responsibility to make their own changes in their life, but also has the ability to do so. So begins a chapter very close to my heart, on a new way of communicating, a new way of listening and relating to one another that can open up possibility in every aspect of your life… coaching.

The word "coach" first appeared in the 1500s and referred to a type of carriage or bus. The etymology of the word "coach" speaks to transporting a person from where she was to where she wanted to go. The profession of coaching, (personal coaching, executive coaching, business coaching, life coaching) that really took hold in the early 1980s, does just that – like a bus, a professional coach is focused on helping her clients move forward to a future that they want for themselves.

At the heart of coaching are a few basic and very simple principles that anyone can begin using at the office or at home, with friends or family, with bosses or co-workers for great effectiveness and improved communication as well as the creation of possibilities.

WHAT IS A COACH APPROACH?

Let me start in a very un-coachy way by talking about what coaching is not. It is not about giving advice or consulting or providing solutions to problems. It is not about mentoring or teaching, and it is not therapy – it is not past-based or working to fix people. Coaching is, by its very nature, agenda-free. Rather than telling and fixing, a coach elicits the client's own action-based solutions.

If you have ever been a supervisor who has always felt you had to have the answers, as I did before I discovered the "coach approach," you will feel an enormous relief at adopting this principle. A coach approach means asking powerful questions to help people figure out what they need rather than telling people what to do. It is liberating to believe your staff person knows the answers and your job is simply to help him or her discover those answers for him or herself.

A coach approach means empowering people to bring their best to the table and gently helps them see their potential as well as their pitfalls so that they can make positive changes in their lives. Using a coach approach with others means that we too are taking accountability and having the courage to look at ourselves and strive for our own full capacity so that we can role model as well as empower. It means we are working toward our own emotional intelligence as well as encouraging its development in others.

WHAT CAN A "COACH APPROACH" DO FOR ME?

Coaching, simply put, is about the other person. By the simple shift of focusing on the other person, one instantly suspends judgment, and the invitation and possibilities for conversation are opened up. By actively listening and really hearing what another is saying, there is an incredible depth of communication that can begin to come into play. How often do you engage in a conversation where you are completely agenda-free?

Often several things are at play for us in a conversation that contributes to getting in the way of listening. We might be sure our point of view is right and need to get that on the table, or we might want to be trying to impress and are thinking of the next thing we will say, or we might be so hell bent on getting our point across that we don't even let the other person finish what they are going to say before jumping in. Being agenda-free is incredibly liberating and by putting yourself in a place of not knowing the right answer, the pressure really disappears.

> It was a huge Aha! moment for the women who attended my workshop on "Adopting a Coach Approach to Life." They realized they are very often in the habit of providing the answer, and of telling or fixing, be it for their staff, their partners, or their children. They began to see how that approach might effectively shut down communication. It was a big eye opener for them to begin experimenting with using a coach approach and resisting the temptation to jump in with the solution or the fix.

WHY DOES COACHING WORK?

Coaching works because the answers come from the individual being coached. They own their answers and are empowered because no external source imposed the ideas that are generated. Coaching gives people emotional ownership, which occurs when they are allowed to be creative and come up with their own solutions. Best of all, coaching leaves people feeling appreciated. To be really heard by someone with no agenda and listened to at the very core of your beliefs and guiding values is a very powerful experience. Coaching is a wondrous human motivator.

WHAT ARE THE BASIC COACHING PRINCIPLES?

The goal of every coaching conversation is for the person being coached to be seen, heard and understood. The coaching principles that seek to have the person you are talking to be seen, heard and understood, take the shift away from our own ego and onto the person to whom we are speaking. Imagine the conversation you could have with someone if you shifted from responding to holding the space for the person so that they can focus on themselves and what is important to them.

BASIC COACHING PRINCIPLES

1. **Trust:** At the core of coaching are trust and the belief that the other person is capable and knows what is best for them.

2. **Curiosity:** In a coaching conversation, it is a time to flex your curiosity muscle, not your knowing muscle. By remaining consistently curious, you keep the possibility potential open. Think of the acronym W.A.I.T. – WHY AM *I* TALKING?

3. **Active Listening:** Active listening is a way of listening that focuses entirely on what the other person is saying and confirms understanding of both the content of the message and the emotions and feelings underlying the message to ensure that understanding is accurate.

   I had a friend who was in the habit of looking around the room and noticing other things when I was engaged in telling her a story. It was most disconcerting, with the result that I never wanted to continue my story. Was she listening? Yes. Was she actively listening? No. Did I feel heard? No. Be aware of how you listen with your friends, your family, your partners and your co-workers. Experiment with active listening and see how your conversations become more connected with the other person.

Active Listening Tips:

- Make eye contact when face-to-face.
- Don't do something else at the same time (e.g., cooking, checking your blackberry, etc.).
- Pay attention and encourage the speaker (nod of the head, "uh huhs," etc.).
- Suspend judgment.
- Be aware of your own biases and eliminate making assumptions.
- Control the need to solve the problem or fix the situation.
- Hold the space for open conversation and don't interrupt.
- Paraphrase what the speaker has said to show you're listening and make sure you have understood correctly.
- Ask questions to clarify for more understanding.
- Provide feedback (see later in this chapter).

Often when we get used to a certain teacher or person talking, the familiarity causes us to cease to listen actively. (I am sure all of you who are parents have experienced this when you ask your kids to get on with their homework. It's strange how they just don't seem to hear after a point.)

It is the bane of a chorus director's existence when they teach a certain principle over and over again and their chorus never seems to permanently adopt it, but then a musical coach comes in from outside and says the same thing and in a heartbeat, the chorus has embraced and incorporated that same technique. With the outside musical coach, the chorus has new ears and they engage in active listening. For the chorus members, the director's and assistant directors' voices (which are heard on a weekly basis) can sometimes become like the incomprehensible "wah wah wah" sounds of the parents' voices in the animated television special, *Charlie Brown's Christmas*.

Master Director, Bobbette Gantz realized she needed to introduce fresh listening ears for her high-level chorus. To increase awareness of the concept of active listening, she started with having the chorus begin to re-listen to the taking of the pitch. When the key was blown on the pitch pipe that became the new prompt for the chorus to make a fresh start to listen actively. In effect Bobbette reframed the taking of the pitch for her chorus as the signal not just to "shush up," but to "step up." Re-tuning the ears helped the chorus become more engaged with hearing the voices of the directors and teaching staff, whom they heard routinely.

Active listening takes energy and thought, and it requires you to be truly present. It requires a shift to the other person. Giving complete attention to the person and what they are saying in the present moment will aid greatly in understanding, and will improve communications in all facets of your life.

THE "COACH" VEHICLE

"always the beautiful answer who asks a more beautiful question"

— e e cummings, poet 1894-1962

The vehicle for creating engaged collaborative conversation is asking effective "Open" questions that invite conversation vs. "Closed" questions that are instant conversation enders. If you incorporate nothing else from this chapter into your communications, I encourage you to begin to adopt more open style questions and notice how that encourages conversation.

Open vs. Closed Questions

Open:
I am curious about…
Can you explain?
I am wondering…
How does _____ work for you?
What do you mean by that?
What did you notice about…?
How does it feel to…?
What would need to be in place for you to…?
How can you…
How will you know if…?

Closed:
Do you think…?
Are you…?
Can you…?
Is there…?
Will you…?
Did you realize that you…?

HOW CAN I INCORPORATE A COACH APPROACH INTO MY LIFE?

In the Home: (experimenting with the coaching goal of having the person to whom you are talking feel seen, heard and understood)

Non-coach approach: (parent is being... well, a parent!)
Teen: "Mom, can I talk to you about something?"
Mom: "Sure, what's up?"
Teen: "I think I want to drop enriched math class."
Mom: (non-coach approach) "But you need that class to get into the "xyz" program at University. If you drop it you won't get in."
Teen: "Well, I am dropping it."
Mom: "You are going to regret it!"
Teen: Leaves the room... conversation ended.

Coach approach: What could happen if the conversation went something like this?
Teen: "Mom, can I talk to you about something?"
Mom: "Sure, what's up?"
Teen: "I want to drop enriched math class."
Mom: (Listens, seeks to clarify) "Oh? What's going on?"
Teen: "Well, I don't like it."
Mom: (seeks to clarify) "What about it don't you like?"
Teen: "It's too hard. I don't get it."
Mom: (seeks to understand) "Hmmm. Are you still enjoying your regular math classes?"
Teen: "Sort of."
Mom: "You sound lukewarm about math... you used to like it a lot – I am wondering what subjects are grabbing your interest more than math these days?"
Teen: "Well, English is okay."
Mom: (conversation continues)

At the Office: (experimenting with open vs. closed questions)

Scenario: Employee is chronically 10-15 min. late in the morning. This has increased in frequency so it is now happening three days a week at least.

There is always a different excuse. Boss is annoyed but hasn't addressed it with Employee yet.

Closed:
Boss: "Are you aware that your shift starts at 9:00 a.m.?"
Employee: "Yes."

Or

Closed:
Boss: "Good morning. You are late again – what happened today?"
Employee: (gives excuse)
Boss: "Well I need you to start work at 9:00 a.m."
Employee: "Okay."
(Note – no possibility for conversation to perhaps get to the root of why employee is habitually late)

Open:
Boss: "Good morning Suzie. How are you?"
Employee: "I am so sorry I am late."
Boss: "I am wondering what happened to you to delay you this morning?" (Note: no judgment, possibilities remain open).
Employee: "Oh, I messed up, I set my clock incorrectly and my alarm didn't go off."
Boss: "That happens. It's ok. I covered for you today. I am noticing that you have been having difficulty getting here on time on a more frequent basis lately."
Employee: "Yeah I know, but I always stay late at night if I arrive late."
Boss: "I know you do, and I appreciate that. You are a hard worker; it's just that your receptionist position does require you to begin answering the phones right when the business opens at 9:00 a.m. and so I really do need you here ready to begin work right at 9:00 a.m. I am wondering what you could do differently or change about your routine to ensure you are punctual?" (dialogue begins)

At Your Rehearsal: (experimenting with a coach approach – suspension of our agenda, opening up possibilities for dialogue, making the other person the focus.)

Scenario:

Christine was absent frequently in the weeks leading up to competition with her demanding out-of-town work and travel schedule. Her riser mates noticed that she was unsure of her choreography moves and was doing several of them incorrectly and they were upset and worried that she wouldn't learn the moves in time. Christine's riser mates might inwardly fume and continually correct her on a frequent basis, which might put Christine on the defensive and feeling bad about herself.

What could happen if Christine's riser mate had had a coaching conversation with her? It could go something like this:

Riser Mate: "Hey, Christine, it's good to see you back on the risers. You have had a crazy schedule with work. I am imagining it must be hard to keep on top of all the chorus changes to the music and choreo. How do you manage?" (note: judgment suspended, understanding exhibited, door is open for Christine)

Christine: "Well, I don't think I am managing very well. I am really worried I won't be able to have it all down correctly by competition time." (Christine shows she is aware of where she is at and she gets to express her fears – she is worried about messing up and letting down the team.)

Riser Mate: "What can I do to help?" (offers support, creates door for possibility)

Christine: "Wow – thanks – I am wondering if you could maybe get together with me to run through the choreo until I get it?"

Riser Mate: "Sure."

REFLECTION QUESTIONS:

1. What might happen if you consciously remained "agenda-free" in a conversation and put the attention on the other person?

2. How could using "open" questions contribute to dialogue?

3. When could you experiment with consciously engaging in active listening?

FEEDBACK

Properly constructed feedback, both given and received, can be one of the most incredible learning gifts we could hope for and an integral part of the coaching journey of positive growth. Often referred to as "Feed Forward," the idea is for feedback to provide an opportunity to learn and grow-so why do we dread getting feedback? Why do the words "Would you like some feedback?" generally strike a horror chord in our hearts? More often than not, it's because feedback, when delivered poorly, feels like a license to be critical. Criticism isn't feedback.

When someone asks for feedback, they may not be asking you to tell them what they did wrong. We presume that we are helping others do better by focusing on pointing out weaknesses, but often the message is received in a way that we did not intend.

For example, you may have wanted to help make my presentation even better by telling me after I spoke, that even though my speech was brilliant and I got a standing ovation, the section where I talked about "goats grazing on fescue" was interminably boring. All you succeeded in doing was to strip me of my standing ovation and the exultation of having delivered a brilliant presentation. How and when those well meaning tidbits are delivered to others needs to be very carefully and systematically considered so that the words are heard in the way you intended.

SETTING THE STAGE

"Without rapport… feedback is just noise."

– Thomas Crane[27]

Setting up a healthy context for giving feedback is critical. A feedback-rich environment needs to be established. The giving and receiving of regular feedback as an opportunity for mutual growth and learning must be accepted and endorsed by all.

Make sure the person is ready to receive feedback. Timing is critical. (For example, if you come up to me right after I have finished the presentation, I may not be in a receptive mood to receive feedback.) Choose a time when both parties are in agreement. Perhaps you might say to me the next day, "I really enjoyed your presentation yesterday and have been thinking about it. Would you like any feedback on your presentation?" (I say, "Sure.")

If you are a boss, setting up a positive atmosphere of growth and learning in advance will ensure that feedback is received more successfully. When I was boss, my staff used to dread the annual performance review until they understood that it was an opportunity for us to talk about mutual goals, about successes and growth opportunities rather than some nitpicky listing of things they did wrong over the past year. Nothing should ever be said in a performance review that the employee is not aware of already. Give the feedback face to face whenever possible.

THE FEEDBACK SANDWICH PRINCIPLE

Kevin Eikenberry[28], noted leadership consultant, has a brilliant and easily understood theory about delivering feedback. He talks about delivering a "Feedback Sandwich." Many of us are familiar with the concept of delivering balanced feedback, although very often, the way it is delivered makes us believe that the real reason the person wanted to give us the feedback was just to let us know what was wrong or needs to be fixed.

---

27 Thomas Crane www.craneconsulting.com
28 Kevin Eikenberry, www.kevineikenberry.com

In a Feedback Sandwich, the sandwich bread is the positive feedback, the things that went well, the good things, and the things that we want to build on. The meat of the sandwich is the stuff that wasn't there, or didn't work well, or the challenge areas.

The trick to preparing an edible feedback sandwich (i.e. one that the person actually wants to eat) is to make sure that you use quality ingredients. We don't seem to have a problem with the insides of the sandwich. Usually the insides are very specific and many-layered. It is rare, however, that we make the bread as specific as the meat.

Does this sound like you? "Great job, Suzie! Now in going through the document – I think that the introduction needs to be shorter and perhaps contain a better indication of what you are trying to say so that you don't lose your audience... and the body lacks flow – I am not really sure what you are trying to say here... and the four key points that I wanted in the report need to be fleshed out a bit. They really aren't clear. Oh yeah, and there are some spelling and grammatical errors as I noted, but, yeah, good effort!"

Yikes! Here is an example where the bread was tasteless and all Suzie would think was that her document sucked. All she would taste were the layers of smoked Italian salami with peppercorns... (the meat, the criticism) – because the meat was specific. Throwing it in between bread was an afterthought. The bread was not specific.

We need to think about making our bread (our "positive feedback") as specific as the meat so the sandwich can be digested. Instead of serving up the three-day old tasteless Wonderbread, think about a sandwich made on lovely rosemary whole-wheat focaccia sprinkled with cheddar and sundried tomatoes with a balsamic drizzle. You get the picture.

What makes a sandwich really edible? You are right, the condiments. I mean, what is a sandwich without the Dijon... the mayo... the pesto spread? The condiments are key to making a feedback sandwich that someone really wants to eat. The condiments are your "intention." It is critical to determine what your intention is for giving feedback before you deliver it.

To take the example of my goats-grazing-on-fescue speech again – the speech was clearly a hit. I got a standing ovation, so why did you want to tell me that one part of the speech was boring? What was your intention in telling me that? Was it to make me feel bad? I doubt it. Was it to make the speech even better so that I am even more successful because you care about me and want me to succeed? Okay, let's think about that one for a second. If the speech was one that I was going to repeat to others, then there might be merit in helping me improve it (with my permission and at the right time). If it was a one-off speech, the only possible thing telling me what was wrong would do, would be to make me feel bad and diminish the success I felt.

By consistently and thoughtfully creating an intention every time you give feedback, you will ensure that you are clear about why you are giving the feedback, and you will add energy to that intention and create a much greater possibility for the feedback to be received.

Always make sure your feedback is lopsided in favor of giving appreciative feedback – Focus on progress, what is going right and what you want more of. Although a sandwich sounds like 2/3 appreciative and 1/3 corrective, Thomas G. Crane,[29] in *The Heart of Coaching*, recommends delivering feedback in an 80/20 ratio – 80% positive and reinforcing, and 20% constructive ideas for change.

Notice that he didn't say 80% positive and 20% negative – even the 20% is framed in an "appreciative" fashion. Instead of saying "I didn't like the section of your presentation where you talked about the goats grazing on fescue – it was boring" – you could say, "The section about the goats grazing could be made more interesting by using some visual aids and adding some humor like you did in the rest of your presentation."

In different situations, it may be appropriate to shift Crane's ratio. In a high-achieving artistic endeavor, the "meat" of the feedback sandwich may be multi-layered and critical to the person's artistic growth. Generally speaking, most high-achievers are keen to know everything that they can do to improve their performance. In all cases, however, it is still critically important to first establish a feedback-receptive environment. Be aware of how you prepare and serve your sandwich to ensure balanced feedback, be sincere, and have a clear intention for giving the feedback so it is heard and received.

---

29 Thomas G. Crane, *The Heart of Coaching* (San Diego: FTA Press, 2002) p. 166

SUMMARY – The Feedback Sandwich

1. Specific, distinctive ingredients (both the bread and the insides)
2. Balance in favor of the "bread" (the appreciative)
3. Don't forget the condiments! (a clear "intention")

In our Barbershop chorus singing culture, members are required to qualify their music by handing in a recording of their voice to an evaluator to ensure a certain standard, before they are allowed to perform publicly or compete with the chorus. The qualification program is pretty much the most stressful part of chorus life for most people. It is important to first set the environment for the program as one of learning and growth for the individual and chorus as a whole.

After an evaluator (Rose) successfully adopted the Feedback Sandwich approach at Lions Gate Chorus, the reaction of the person being evaluated (Dawn) was quite different than it had been in the past.

"Wow," said Dawn, "Rose said I had a really lovely quality to my voice. No one has ever said that before. Oh yeah, there were a few notes wrong and stuff I have to work on rhythmically, but I don't suck! I feel great!"

REFLECTION QUESTIONS:

1. What steps could you take to create an environment open to giving and receiving feedback as a method of growth and learning at work, at home, at your chorus rehearsal?

2. Where in your life do you give "criticism" under the guise of "feedback"?

3. How could adding the condiments (your intention) transform the kind of feedback you give and how you give it?

4. What might happen if you started giving a "Feedback Sandwich?"

9

DO-ABLE GOAL SETTING
The Power of
Incremental Improvement

"Motivation is an external, temporary high that PUSHES you forward. Inspiration is a sustainable internal glow which PULLS you forward."

– Thomas Leonard[32]

o-able goal setting – huh? Isn't that an oxymoron? Doesn't that mean you have set your goal too small? I realize I am speaking to the high achievers reading this, those whose goals are no doubt nothing less than solving world hunger. Does the very thought of setting goals make you tired? "Yeah, Jan, I know that we are all supposed to set goals in order to go anywhere or to move forward or to achieve... but why can't we just 'be'?" Fair enough! Life does not have to be a series of conquests, and, as we have discovered throughout this book, it is vitally important to be content where you are right now in order to achieve inner harmony.

Let's say that you are absolutely content and completely at peace and in harmony with every part of your life right now. There is absolutely nothing you feel that you would like to work toward, nothing at all you feel driven to do, either for yourself, your family or the community at large. If that is the case, flip to the next chapter and begin your celebrating!

For the rest of you, read on. I imagine you have read hundreds of articles on goal setting throughout your life and set thousands of goals for yourselves

---

32 Thomas Leonard, Founder, CoachVille.com. For more information, visit www.BestofThomas.com

that you have either achieved, partially achieved, gotten tired of working on and abandoned, or actually never took any action toward at all.

I believe that setting goals consistently and methodically, working towards them, re-evaluating and then re-setting those goals, are key to achieving success in life (whatever your definition of success is). Without setting goals, life just "happens" without any real purpose or direction. Days, months, even years can drift by. The positive results of making progress on and achieving goals are significant. Think of the sense of satisfaction you have when you finally cleaned out your closets and donated the clothing that hasn't fit you since high school. Think of the confidence you got when you returned intact from your first solo traveling adventure. Think of how much easier it was to make your *second* presentation in front of senior management.

> One of the choruses with whom I worked had experienced what they considered a disastrous failure by not achieving a competition goal they had set for themselves. The fallout was tremendous for them – not only had they let their goal define them as a group, but also they were so intimately connected and intertwined with it that not to reach their goal felt to them as if they were failures – both individually and as a chorus. The instant reaction by many was to assign blame and there were many different opinions of who to assign that blame to. This was a crisis for the group, it fractured them, pitted sub-groups against each other and after months of painful working through the divisiveness, they managed to begin to rebuild. The chorus, however, then went into a period of timidity – of not wanting to set any goals for fear they might not achieve them and would be burned again. In a sense, the chorus was adrift – if there were no goals, why were they working so hard? Why were they rehearsing weekly and spending thousands of dollars on hiring coaches? We spent some time together in a safe environment working through creation of new group goals that all could share and embrace without fear, and the chorus is now well on the way toward that new path of possibility.

My goal is to create some simple possibilities for you to not only create goals for yourself, but also to show you a simple step-by-step way to achieve them.

GETTING STARTED – CREATION OF GOALS – Three Easy Steps

1. Start here: The "Black and White"

Although the first use of the term S.M.A.R.T. goals is unknown, and although there are many slight variations, the principles remain the same.

S.M.A.R.T. GOALS –

- **S**pecific (What exactly is your goal? Goals are no place to be vague.)
- **M**easurable (How will you measure it?)
- **A**ttainable (By breaking the goal down, is it attainable?)
- **R**ealistic (Is this a goal that you honestly are willing to work toward?)
- **T**imely (When will you achieve it? Set a time frame.)

Set yourself up for success by choosing S.M.A.R.T. goals. One of the biggest ways to bag out of achieving a goal is to make it too big and too vague. For example, "I am going to get fit in 2009." What does that mean? Does "fit" mean percentage body fat, heart rate, how long I exercise, a feeling of well-being? Being 100% clear about what the goal actually is and what you really want is critical to the goal planning process.

2. Add this: The "Color"

On paper it all looks good. You have created a list of S.M.A.R.T. goals; sounds good, very linear, and eminently sensible. The thing that will give your goal that extra life and that extra humanness is to relate those goals to your feelings. Your motivation, your "why" behind the goal is really critical to your success in achieving your goals. The "why" of your goals must connect and be consistent with your values.

If you feel one of those nasty "shoulds" slide in there, take a long hard look at your statement – e.g., I "should get fit for health reasons." Ask yourself: "Why do I want to get fit?" "I want to get fit so that I am healthier, and live longer so I can see my grandchildren grow up." Isn't that more powerful? Make sure that the goals are yours and not someone else's!

Add in as much color as you can by using your five senses. What would achieving your goal look like, feel like, sound like, taste like, smell like? Adding in the sensory elements will add a layer of passion and excitement to your goal.

Let's try it out with the previous example:

My goal: To get fit in 2009
What does that look like? (I can run 10 km at more than a jog without stopping)
What does it feel like? (easy, exhilarating, strong, coordinated, lean)
What does it sound like? (Zen-like peacefulness in my head)
What does it smell like? (outdoors, fresh sea air on the seawall)
What does it taste like? (salty sweat)

By adding my five senses to create a living, breathing feeling of my goal, I have made it very, very real. That gives me a very powerful possibility to live into.

3. Then… Make it Real – Write it down.

"Goals in writing are dreams with deadlines."

– Brian Tracy[33]

It has been proven that to write down our goals and record our progress keeps our goals top of mind, keeps us focused, and can have a huge impact on our results. Brian Tracy, motivational author and guru, says that only about 3% of adults write their goals down and that those people accomplished many times as much as people who don't.

It is no accident that Running Journals have Running Logs included in the content program, and add descriptors such as: what was the weather like, the slope, etc., to make it more colorful and real, so go and buy yourself a journal or a notebook, and start keeping track of your successes.

Make this a daily practice – re-read, recommit and track progress to your goals every day.

---

33 Brian Tracy, www.briantracy.com

EXERCISE: GOAL CREATION

The Black & White (S.M.A.R.T. GOAL)	The Why	The Color (look, feel, sound, smell, taste)

ACTION PLANNING – Three Easy Steps

1. The Long List – Brainstorm

Brian Tracy suggests brainstorming a "Long List" of everything you can possibly think of that you can do to help yourself achieve your goal. By doing this, you open up infinite possibilities and actions that might move you forward toward your goals; some of which may not have immediately come to mind when you first created that goal.

2. The Increments – Choose and Create

From your "Long List," choose the top three things you feel will make the most difference and propel you the fastest toward your goals. Create a clear series of actionable objectives on how you will proceed toward those three sub-goals. When you break your long-range goals into actionable increments, be sure that each piece is kept bite–sized. Set yourself up for success and at least one daily victory!

3. The Commitment

A goal without an action plan is just a good idea. Make the commitment to reach your goal. Have an honest talk with yourself and ask yourself if you are committed to reaching your goals. Be clear and realistic about what might get in the way. If your goal needs to be revised, revise it and carry on.

EXERCISE: ACTION PLANNING WORKSHEET

S.M.A.R.T. GOAL	THE LONG LIST	THE INCREMENTS	THE COMMITMENT

HOW TO KEEP GOING – Three Easy Ways

1. Support

What and who will support you? What qualities do you have in yourself to draw on and support you? (e.g., motivation, drive, etc.) Which people will honestly be supportive of your goal?

Be careful with whom you share your goals. Sometimes those closest to us may not give us the greatest amount of support because they are fearful of what your change might mean for them.

What resources do you have to support you? (community, equipment, etc.)

2. Accountability

Have you made a contract with yourself, or with someone else? Find someone who will support your goals. Give them specific instructions on how you want to be held accountable.

For instance, in the writing of the first draft of this book I had two accountability partners – my coach, and a trusted friend. I gave them a schedule of when I would deliver chapters to them and if I didn't they were instructed to give me a hard time; to question me, to get me to recommit to when I would deliver a chapter. Having to be accountable drove my writing. I imagined my accountability partners sitting by their computers anxiously waiting for the latest chapter to come in. I couldn't disappoint them!

3. Rewards

I strongly believe in rewarding oneself when one achieves a milestone – or even gets bite-sized tasks completed. What that reward is can be as individual as you are. I rely heavily on a "sticker" system for my bite-sized goals.

> Coach Laura West[34] relies on her "giggle goals." "One of my favorite systems is my Daily Giggle Goals. Each day I sit down as I'm planning out my priorities for the day and I pick three goals (bite-sized is key) to get done today. These are three things that would have me smile and giggle with delight at the end of the day when I know they are done."

---

34 Laura West, *Center for Joyful Business* www.JoyfulBusiness.com

For bigger achievements a reward might mean a night off without work or a nice dinner out – whatever works for you. The point is to create a reward system to keep you going and to motivate you. I know that when I achieve my goal of finishing writing this chapter I can go and sit on my deck chaise and have a glass of wine. I am motivated!

EXERCISE: HOW TO KEEP GOING

SUPPORTS (internal, external)	ACCOUNTABILITY (who, how)	REWARDS (what, when)

HOW TO GET PAST THE ROADBLOCKS

Sometimes it may seem like the universe is conspiring to take you off your "road to success." Here are a few ideas for ways to navigate around the potholes that get in the way.

Forks in the Road

Hitting an unforeseen fork in the road may require one to revise a goal. That's okay! Think of revision as an opportunity that indicates you have received new insight about a previously held goal.

Switchbacks

The road to your goal may not be a straight one. There is a reason switchbacks were created on the mountainside. Sometimes going straight up is just too difficult. Remember – every step you take gets you closer to your goal. Celebrate each "switchback" – celebrate each fork in the road, each step closer to your goal. The entire hill does not have to be scaled in one go-round.

Dead Ends

Eek! Did you hit a dead end? Turn around and retrace your steps. Go back to your LONG LIST (or see p. 125) and travel a new route.

Overcoming Obstacles

> *"Obstacles are those dreadful things you see when*
> *you take your eyes off your goals."*
>
> – Henry Ford

Take the inspirational story of John Di Lemme. John was clinically diagnosed as a stutterer at a young age and told he would never speak fluently. He describes himself as an *"Obstacle Overcomer"* and says, *"Obstacles are the enemy trying to keep you down. When you decide to face the obstacle, you head into the Promised Land."* [35] He is now changing lives worldwide as a renowned

---

35 John Di Lemme, www. ChampionsLiveFree .com

international motivational speaker with a passion for teaching others how to live a champion life despite the label society has placed on them.

Ask yourself: Is it an obstacle or an excuse?

The Road is Too Steep and I just have to rest.

That's okay! When you do rest, be sure to do as they do on San Francisco's incredibly steep hills – Curb your wheels. By "curbing your wheels" you will ensure you don't backslide. When you are ready to move again, just switch into gear, release your emergency brake and gun it full speed ahead!

THE POWER OF INCREMENTAL IMPROVEMENT

"Your short–term actions multiplied by time equals
your long–term accomplishments."

– Denis Waitley[36]

Although there is nothing more satisfying and motivating than visibly see-ing big leaps forward on your goal-o-meter, getting addicted to the big push can run counter to all of the amazing progress you are making daily.

Ultimately, you want to move forward toward achieving your goals. My thesis is that *any* step forward is an improvement over where you were before. "The Power of Incremental Improvement" is easily applicable to your indi-vidual goals. There is a certain momentum that is built simply by ticking off the signposts along the way. It is important to keep track of the strides you make, however big or small they are. They all contribute to the overall goal.

The exciting thing is that in a group or team situation, this "Power of Incremental Improvement" becomes exponential – much like the measure-ments of an earthquake. Groups with a clear, concise, common goal can achieve miraculous results by each member of the group moving forward toward the group goal in whatever measure they can achieve individually.

When preparing for 2009 International Competition, Lions Gate Chorus adopted a "One More Point" program in the month before the competition. The premise of this program was: "What would you be will-ing to do if it meant you could get one more point for the chorus?" For others that meant adding a couple of days of exercise per week to increase their stamina. For still others it meant asking their families for support so that their mental stress was reduced. For some it meant ensuring that they attended extra choreography sessions. Each person and each action was important and could make a difference.

One More Point – by itself seems small. Multiplied by 120 people could mean the difference between a bronze and gold medal: The Power of Incremental Improvement!

---

36 Denis Waitley, best-selling author, speaker and success coach www.deniswaitley.com

STAGE A HIT OF MASSIVE ACTION

Noted leadership coach, Kevin Eikenberry,[37] believes we must not only approach achieving goals with incremental improvement, but also must stage sessions of "massive action" in order to create momentum and make big progress. Along with your incremental steps, dream big, and plan for a radical hit of "massive action."

> *"If you ever think you're too small to make a difference, try going to bed with a mosquito in the room."*
>
> – Dame Anita Roddick, environmentalist and founder of the Body Shop

37 www.kevineikenberry.com

WHAT TO DO WHEN YOU GET THERE (OR NOT!)

I guess I should have called this section "What to do *before* you get there" because pre-planning for the part that comes after the goal being achieved or not is very important. Whether we reach or don't quite reach our goal, there are fallouts and we must prepare in advance for them.

The celebratory part may sound easy, but all too often, we rush head-long into thinking about the next goal before taking the time to celebrate and close off the goal just achieved. Even with an achieved goal, as an individual, you may feel a gamut of emotions ranging from elation, to depression, even to fear. Expect the unexpected and you probably will be prepared. For individuals, it is a perfect time to re-group and re-assess.

In a group setting, those effects are magnified and even more varied, whether a goal is achieved, or not. There are a few steps that are key to institute so you have a place to go on the morning after your big celebration. Allow yourself and your team to spend the time they need on celebrating their achievement before you go screaming off into the next stretch goal. Consistently put value on the goal you have achieved by recognizing it, and the people involved in creating it.

As a leader in a group setting be sure to stay aware of how your team is feeling and acting. Create an environment that allows for open dialogue without judgment. Let everyone express their feelings, and listen to them without trying to heal them.

Let time pass and know that there may be a period of disinterest, lethargy, or fatigue with your team. If a goal has been missed, it is a fabulous learning opportunity for the group to allow the time for reflection and discussion of what happened – what went well, what could be changed for the next time. It is time then to re-assess and re-commit to another goal, building on the success of the past, and then look higher to a brand new beginning.

Perdita Felicien is a Canadian world-champion hurdler who was heavily favored to win the gold medal in the 100-meter hurdles at the 2004 summer Olympics in Athens.

The hopes of a nation were on her, expectations were high and the pressure was incredible. In the final race, she dramatically hit the first hurdle and fell hard, taking herself out of the race and shattering her Olympic gold medal dreams. At that moment, she was devastated. She had been training hard for that moment every day for years and in a heartbeat, the moment was gone.

After reflection, she talked to reporters and said "I have learned not to define myself by one event, no matter how big. My self-worth is not dependent on an event that lasts less than 13 seconds. Hurdling is what I do, it is not what defines me. That is why I know, in this challenging time, I will emerge better (for having struggled) and thrive once again."

Perdita left a fine reminder to all of us – we are who we are, not what we do.

10

YEAH, BABY, YOU ARE WORTH IT
Celebration and Acknowledgement

*"I am what I am
I am my own special creation"*

– Gloria Gaynor, from the song, *"I Am What I Am"*

I can feel a lot of you cringing when I ask you to even consider celebrating and acknowledging yourselves. Most of us were taught that modesty and self-effacement are desirable qualities, and to boast or brag about one's accomplishments is, well, just not done. Some of you may think it is selfish, or unseemly to think about or talk about yourself. When was the last time you really acknowledged yourself, not for an event, or something you did but for who you are? When did you last say, "Hey, (insert your name here), you are a really terrific person."? In order truly to achieve harmony from the inside out, we must learn to really recognize, own and celebrate what is inside.

If by chance you are one of those rare individuals who has no issues with accepting, acknowledging and regularly celebrating your brilliance, then you may want to skip right to the end of this chapter. (Oh, and by the way, congratulations! You are amazing!)

I facilitate a popular workshop for women called the "Celebrate Yourself Night" that begins with wine and chocolate and heads into a three-hour workshop of celebrating each person's individual fabulousness. It is common for everyone to start the evening with a lot of quiet hesitation, trepidation and embarrassment. Even the thought of talking about themselves is difficult for many. By the end of the night the decibel level in the room has increased to an almost deafening level and the incredibly good feeling of being able to be completely real in their skins is liberating and makes them want to shout!

At the end of one workshop, a top CEO in a local corporation, when asked what she was taking away from the workshop, said, "Now I feel like I have worth." Imagine that! She got an instant feeling of self-worth not from running a multi-million dollar corporation, but by an evening spent recognizing and acknowledging her own unique gifts in a trusting atmosphere.

Acknowledging and celebrating our own gifts simply makes us feel good. The entire harmony from the Inside Out approach is to work from our strengths to amplify and magnify what is already good and thereby make it great. The awareness of what those strengths are is critical to move forward. In a moment we can shift from scarcity thinking (what is wrong with us) to abundance thinking (what is right with us). As we saw in chapter one, by working from the appreciative approach we create unlimited possibilities for our lives and ourselves. If your duck is still yammering on about how selfish it is to think of oneself, consider this: the appreciative approach would indicate that, by acknowledging and working from our strengths, we can become the best we possibly can be, and by achieving our peak potential we can contribute even more to the world. It is really an unselfish act – playing small and/or downplaying our attributes serves absolutely no one. Playing to our strengths means we can give more.

Let's get started!

First up – It's time to take stock. You may not run around talking about your signature strengths, but are you even aware of what they are? Can you celebrate your own fabulousness? Take a moment to think about those personal qualities of which you are most proud. What do you love about you? How would you want to hear yourself described in a eulogy?

EXERCISE:
CELEBRATE YOURSELF – TWENTY in THREE!

Let your mind go. Now write down twenty things you love about yourself (in no particular order). Set the timer to three minutes. Go!

1.	
2.	
3.	
4.	
5.	
6.	
7.	
8.	
9.	
10.	
11.	
12.	
13.	
14.	
15.	
16.	
17.	
18.	
19.	
20.	

REFLECTION QUESTIONS:

1. Did you finish your list of 20 things? If so, jump to # 3.

2. If you didn't finish your list, your homework is to finish it! Stuck? Ask a good friend what fabulous qualities they see in you that you have omitted.

3. Once you finish, grab a friend or partner and read your list out loud to them. How did that feel? Did you speed up or slow down? Were some things easier to say than others? Did you find yourself justifying your points? E.g., I am good-natured… (me justifying – well I think I am most days.)

4. Keep your list handy so you can read it often to remind yourself of your fabulousness.

THE FOOTBALL FIELD PRINCIPLE

I do a lot of coaching work with high-achievers, and have found that not only do they generally exhibit the inability to celebrate their own gifts, but they also have difficulty celebrating their accomplishments. This has led me to develop what I call "The Football Field Principle."

The Football Field Principle was developed from something very profound that a wise job counselor I went to in the 90s said to me that ultimately has radically shaped my life. After listening to my history and doing a number of "assessments," he looked me straight in the eye and said that I needed to understand that I am playing on a different length of football field. I waited until he explained. "Well," he said, "a normal US football field is 100 yards long. For whatever reason, you have decided that you are playing on a 150-yard field. That means that when, by the actual rules of the game, you get a touchdown, you think you still have 50 yards to go!"

The upside to that: You are highly motivated to do even more.

The downside: You never ever celebrate the touchdowns you *do* achieve because you think you still have 50 yards to go!

The danger in playing on a longer than normal football field is that we spend our lives thinking that there is something else that we have to do, something else we have to achieve in order to "make it." That has a direct impact on our peace and contentment and with just being where we are right here… and right now.

REFLECTION QUESTIONS:

1. What is the length of your football field and how does that play out in your life?

2. Is there somewhere in your life where you are not giving yourself a break?

3. Is there somewhere in your life where you are not celebrating the touchdowns you have achieved?

CREATING YOUR LIFE TOUCHDOWN LIST

Along with celebrating your unique gifts and skills, it is also time to celebrate the incredible amount of things you have already achieved in your lifetime. A touchdown doesn't need to be of Nobel Prize winning magnitude. It can be a personal triumph like finishing a 10 km run or as simple (now I didn't say "easy") as getting the kids off to school with their lunches and homework intact, or perhaps your ongoing triumph as a teacher who inspires your students.

I challenge *you* to challenge your idea of what a touchdown is. Are you playing by a different set of rules? Are you okay with changing those rules?

Look at the following time periods of your life and write at least three "TOUCHDOWNS" for each period of your life.

EXERCISE: MY TOUCHDOWN LIST

Childhood:

1.
2.
3.

Young Adult:

1.
2.
3.

Adult:

1.
2.
3.

In the Past Year:

1.
2.
3.

In the Past Week:

1.
2.
3.

EXERCISE: MY ONGOING TOUCHDOWN LIST

Start noting your touchdowns as they occur. Celebrate your own
victories on an ongoing basis.

1.	
2.	
3.	
4.	
5.	
6.	
7.	
8.	
9.	
10.	
11.	
12.	
13.	
14.	
15.	
16.	
17.	
18.	
19.	
20.	

THE POWER OF ACKNOWLEDGEMENT

Now that we have learned some new skills in appreciating and acknowledging our achievements, and ourselves, it is time to look outward – outward from our inner skills and attributes – and open up to the world at large. Acknowledging and appreciating others is key to the creation of successful relationships. To give freely to others, making them feel appreciated and acknowledged, is one of the greatest keys to a happy and fulfilled life. By affirming and acknowledging what others are doing right, we will ensure that they do more of it. It's just that simple. Different from feedback, acknowledgement and appreciation are just pure, clean, simple and honest ways to say, "Hey, I noticed, I appreciate that and I want to acknowledge that." Thomas Leonard[38], founder of the International Coach Federation said, *We need to remind people of who they are as well as just complimenting them on what they have done.*

Just to clear up any misconception: high-achievers and those working at a high degree of mastery need authentic and sincere acknowledgement too!

KEY POINTS TO GIVING ACKNOWLEDGEMENT

Frequency: Do it often. Once a year at a performance review will not cut it. The more you give acknowledgement, the more natural you will be in giving it. Give yourself a goal of once per day to start.

Be specific: "Good job," although friendly, won't be remembered. "Congratulations on the good job figuring out the details of the June account transfers. That was really complex and you really were incredibly accurate and thorough," will hit the mark.

Be sincere: If it sounds false to you, it will sound false to the receiver.

Make sure that it is heard: Receiving acknowledgement is uncomfortable for many. If you get brushed off, or if the person tries to downplay it, keep at it. Restate your acknowledgement until you are sure they have heard it. In my experience, it often takes three or more times until the person hears the acknowledgement. (See next page for an example of "layered acknowledgement.")

Frequency: Do it often! (Oh, did I say that already?) ☺

---

38 Thomas Leonard, Founder, CoachVille.com. For more information, visit www.BestofThomas.com

LAYERED ACKNOWLEDGEMENT:

Layering your acknowledgement is a wonderful strategy to utilize for those who are having difficulty "hearing" and receiving your acknowledgement. When you restate the acknowledgement after you are brushed off, add to it – in effect, if you think of it like a tiered cake, you are continuing to enhance the acknowledgement by adding tiers of words that add even more color to your statement.

Example:
ME: "Thank you for the great job you did on the organization of Cindy's retirement party. Everyone had a great time."
YOU: "Oh it was nothing. I enjoyed doing it for her." (Common brush-off #1: I enjoyed doing it so do not deserve acknowledgement)

or

YOU: "Oh it was nothing – it didn't take me any time at all." (Common brush-off #2: because I didn't find it difficult to do I do not deserve acknowledgement)
ME: (adding a second tier) "Still – I really appreciate your fine attention to detail – it was very important to me and the company to really acknowledge Cindy's contribution in a classy and lasting way and you clearly put a lot of thought and effort into making it an evening Cindy will always remember, from the detail on the personalized décor to the incredible sculpture you picked out as a gift. We all really want to thank you for a stellar organizing job."
YOU: "Well, I can't believe I forgot to..." (Common brush-off #3: downplaying the achievement by pointing out the mistakes)
ME: "Oh, no one noticed that – they were having so much fun dancing. You know, you have a combination of a lot of unique qualities – your creativity and organizational skills really made the event a success – I can't think of anyone else who could have done it as well. Thank you."
YOU: "Thank you." (Finally!)

RECEIVING ACKNOWLEDGEMENT

Another key skill is the ability to receive acknowledgement. This skill of being able to receive acknowledgement is fundamental to the ability to give it meaningfully. When someone acknowledges you, listen and thank them. Acceptance of their acknowledgement validates the giver. Give them the gift of that feeling.

EXERCISE: RECIPROCAL ACKNOWLEDGEMENT

This exercise is excellent because it combines self-acknowledgement with acknowledgement of others. Do this one with your family, with your workmates, with your chorus riser mates.

PERSON "A" tells PERSON "B" one thing that they are proud of that they bring to the family, the company workplace, to the chorus environment. PERSON "B" listens.
PERSON "B" acknowledges PERSON "A" for whatever that thing is.
PERSON "B" can add more color, to even more deeply acknowledge PERSON "A's" contribution.

Example (Family):
WIFE says to husband: "I am really proud of the way I manage my multi-tasking so well; of juggling my work, of running the household and being a mom."
HUSBAND acknowledges: "I would like to acknowledge you for the incredible work you do. First of all, you get up first in the morning, and make all of the lunches before you rush off to your workplace that I know is hugely demanding, and then you pick up the kids and get them started on their homework and get dinner started before I even get home. My commute is so long and I am so tired, that to come home to a happy home with kids happy and a lovely smell of cooking in the air makes me really feel blessed. I really want to let you know how much that means to me and how much I appreciate that."
WIFE: "Thank you."

THE POWER OF GRATITUDE

DEVELOPING A GRRR-ATTITUDE!

Remember Tony the Tiger? You know: the advertising cartoon mascot for Kellogg's Frosted Flakes cereal with the deep bass voice who wasn't afraid to let us know that Frosted Flakes were "Grrr-eat!"

Science has now confirmed that gratitude is good for your health. A practice of gratitude changes our neural pathways establishing a neural groove that actually makes us feel better! Gratitude is a high vibrational energy. Being in appreciation means you have no resistance. You are allowing life in fully and are aligned with what is happening.

Imagine what could happen if we approached our lives like Tony the Tiger approached his bowl of Frosted Flakes. Gratitude is an attitude. Gratitude is a choice, and… gratitude can become a habit. Like Tony the Tiger would do, let's turn "gratitude" into GRRR-ATTITUDE!

> *"Gratitude unlocks the fullness of life. It turns what we have into enough, and more. It turns denial into acceptance, chaos into order, confusion into clarity… It turns problems into gifts, failures into success, the unexpected into perfect timing and mistakes into important events. Gratitude makes sense of our past, brings peace for today, and creates a vision for tomorrow."*
>
> – Melodie Beattie[39]

Three ways Grrr-Attitude will change your life

1. You will find that *Grrr-Attitude* expands; the more gratitude you have, the more you have to be grateful for!
2. *Grrr-Attitude* positive-izes your focus. *Grrr-Attitude* instantly changes your thinking from a place of scarcity to a place of plenty.
3. *Grrr-Attitude* helps you slow down and enjoy life, which reduces stress and improves your relationships.

---

39 Melody Beattie, author www.melodybeattie.com

DEVELOPING YOUR GRRR-ATTITUDE:

1. Make a Grrr- Attitude List

I invite you to create an ongoing list of the things in your life for which you are grateful. Have some fun with this! Get a big poster board and have your entire family contribute.

> An elementary school principal whom I coached, created a "Gratitude Wall" on one of the student bulletin boards at the school entrance. Students were encouraged to bring in photos, or add words or images of things they were grateful for in their lives. What started as a one-month project was so popular that they kept it up and kept adding to it for the entire school year.

2. Take part in a daily "Grrr-Attitude" challenge

Here's the challenge – make a conscious effort to acknowledge and appreciate at least three people per day. Express your gratitude. Go public with your thoughts. I guarantee you will make someone's day. Try to go even one step further than "Thank you." E.g., when speaking to the Safeway cashier, "Wow! You are really busy. I am impressed that you keep your cool and are pleasant when you are under so much pressure. Thank you."

3. Take part in a nightly "Grrr-Attitude" sign-off

Spend five minutes just before you fall asleep writing down what happened or what you noticed that day for which you are grateful. You will find that you will begin to be more aware of and thankful for the small things (the little girl next door who smiled at you), small victories (like getting the Christmas tree lights untangled), as well as the bigger things (I am grateful that I a roof over my head in this blizzard). You will go to sleep with positive thoughts and *Grrr-Attitude* rather than thoughts of worry and stress.

EXERCISE: MY GRRR-ATTITUDE LIST
What are you grateful for?

1.	
2.	
3.	
4.	
5.	
6.	
7.	
8.	
9.	
10.	
11.	
12.	
13.	
14.	
15.	
16.	
17.	
18.	
19.	
20.	

CELEBRATING THE SUCCESS OF OTHERS

This may be the toughest section to swallow of this entire book and if you ever find yourself falling into the trap or mind-set of "comparison" with accompanying feelings of upset, insecurity and envy, then this also may be the biggest learning "edge" to shift your happiness quotient.

"Comparison is the thief of joy."

– C.S. Lewis

Truer words were never spoken. As long as you view life as a competition – with one person's victory meaning a "loss" for you, your joy and happiness will be seriously compromised. And, as we discussed in Chapter Two, you are creating mental interference that will affect you achieving your performance potential.

Remember, when you actually are in a competition setting – those feelings of jealousy and fear about a competitor's achievements *are getting in the way* of your own success. In fact, the only thing you can control is your own performance and your own mental and emotional state. In a competitive environment (aka the world we live in), we cannot control what others do, or how well they do. To obsess about that is, in effect, obsessing over things that we cannot control, and that we cannot change.

Master Director, Jim Arns, of the Melodeers Chorus (five time International Chorus Champions), told Lions Gate Chorus at their final coaching session before the 2007 International Chorus Competition in Calgary, "If you sing like that and don't make the Top Ten, then I want you to go up to every person in choruses who did make the Top Ten and shake their hands because they did really really well."

He was in fact saying to us that we had the potential and the skills to achieve our Top Ten goal. The parts we were in control of were in place, but we had no control over what would happen with our competitors and should we sing the way we had just sung for him (i.e. at a Top Ten level of excellence) and not make the Top

Ten, that we should just congratulate our competitors who had raised the bar even further. It was a wonderful way to frame our achievement as a chorus and to put the competition scenario in an objective light.

Thematic throughout this book is the concept of looking for the good, working from the positive, finding joy and pleasure in what we have, and not focusing on what we don't have. If someone you know has a success that you do not – gets a great job, gets engaged, wins a competition – ask yourself how you could genuinely share in their success and be happy for them. Ask yourself how you would want them to feel if you were the one having the success. Create an affirmation of "blessing the competition." You and your life will be happy you did.

"The people who have achieved more than you, in any area, are only a half step ahead of you in time. Bless them and praise their gifts, and bless and praise your own. The world would be less rich without their contributions, and it would be less rich without yours. There's more than room for everyone; in fact, there's a need for everyone."

– Marianne Williamson[40]

---

40 Marianne Williamson, *A Return to Love – Reflections on the Principles of A Course in Miracles* (Harper Collins, New York, 1993) p. 222

CONCLUSION

S o where do you go from here? This book has supplied you with a lot of concepts and information, and my hope is that they resonated with you and you now have some practical ways to work from the inside out to achieve harmony in your life.

To recap the Inner Coaching process – we began with the Appreciative Approach and you saw how a simple shift in where you place your mental focus can make a huge difference in your life. Getting rid of the interferences, both external and mental, and creating a context of positivity in which to work, opened you up for using the mind, grounding and visualization techniques to maximize your awareness and ability to be present. You learned how to add energy to any action simply by holding an intention for it. You got a taste of how to begin incorporating some of the basic principles of the coaching profession into your life, and learned some techniques for making goal setting do-able. You saw, how by celebrating and acknowledging yourself and owning and living into your strengths and achievements, you could experience enhanced success and make a greater life contribution.

What are the next steps? First of all, I recommend getting support – a friend, a coach, a partner – someone who is committed to your learning and growth. Look back through the book and decide which concepts, when implemented, will make the most positive difference in your life immediately. Review your best next steps with your buddy. Remember the power of incremental improvement – any step you take will move you forward. As you begin to feel the benefits of working from the inside out, you will want to incorporate as many of those principles as possible into your life. You can access your inner brilliance any time you choose. Sometimes the work may feel uncomfortable, and sometimes you may feel resistance. Just notice and acknowledge those feelings and then give them a good old "heave ho" and carry on.

I truly believe that these "Inner Coaching" principles, when applied to any part of your life or work, will help create transformative change.

Holding a positive attitude and commitment to live authentically is guaranteed to bring you unbridled joy (and a heck of a lot of laughter)!

I look forward to toasting your success as you live into your potential and achieve harmony from the inside out.

ACKNOWLEDGEMENTS

I have been truly inspired and supported by so many people, without whom, this book never could have been written; to all of you, my heartfelt gratitude.

First and foremost, I would like to thank the amazing women of Lions Gate Chorus. They were, in a sense, my "guinea pigs," and willingly put themselves in my hands to test out the principles I have described in this book. Led by their one-of-a-kind Master Director, Sandy Marron, they willingly experimented and embraced the concepts that would help lead them to achieve their peak potential as a chorus and as human beings.

Thanks to all of the other directors and chorus members with whom I have worked over the past two years, who gave of themselves so willingly. Each of you contributed and helped shape this book in so many ways. You made me believe that what I had to say could help others – the way it has helped you – and that I absolutely *must* write a book!

Thank you to all of my coaching clients whose commitment to personal growth and whose amazing journeys continue to inspire me. Thanks to my coaching colleagues and other professionals, who do amazing work to better the lives of others and inspired me and/or allowed me to use their quotes and content in this book. I encourage you to visit their websites and read their books.

To my coach, Lesley-Ann Marriott, who believed in me more than I think I believed in myself; to my mentor, Carollyne Conlinn, for inspiring and encouraging me to be the coach that I am today; to my "woo woo" teachers, Bea Woloshen and Vi Feist, I thank you all from the bottom of my heart. To my fabulous baritone proofreader, Joy Bruce, who really did make sure I dotted my i's and crossed my t's, thank you – your attention to detail is amazing!

Thank you to all of the people who generously contributed their stories and/or who gave me input and assistance in editing and shaping this book:

Meghan Fell, Donna Binder, Kay MacDierney, Sally Griffiths, Betsy Long, Daryl Harmer, Julie Terpenning, Sandy Marron, Julie Starr, Bobbette Gantz, Ryan Heller, Dawn McKenna, Jim Arns, Dave Carley, Cindy Gauthier, Cammi and Don MacKinlay, David Mollenhauer, Carollyne Conlinn, Vi Feist, Bea Woloshen. Special thanks to my brother, Gord Carley, for his valuable advice and ongoing guidance in helping me wend my way through the self-publishing world.

Profuse thanks are sent to Jeff Lewis and Allison Prinsen of me&lewis ideas inc. for so generously and enthusiastically creating the awesome book cover design. Huge gratitude goes out to my very patient book designer, Deb Carfrae of DLC Designs, for creating an absolutely stunning layout. Thanks to Jorge, at Friesens, for answering all of my nine million questions about book printing.

Last, but not least, my love and unending gratitude is sent to my son, Liam, for his wise-beyond-his-years support, and my parents: my mother, Mig, and my late father, Robert, who instilled in me the perspective of "anything being possible for anyone." That belief allowed me to forge this wonderful new coaching career at mid-life and has formed the critical foundation of my coaching philosophy.

RESOURCES &
RECOMMENDED WEBSITES

The following books and people inspired me in the writing of this book. I encourage you to visit their websites and support their work.

The Appreciative Inquiry Commons – a worldwide portal to share information on Appreciative Inquiry and the rapidly growing discipline of positive change. ■ http://appreciativeinquiry.case.edu

Barry Green and Timothy Gallwey, *The Inner Game of Music* ■ www.innergameofmusic.com

Kevin Eikenberry, Chief Potential Officer, The Kevin Eikenberry Group ■ www.kevineikenberry.com

Suzanne Zeman, *Listening to Bodies – A Somatic Primer for Coaches, Managers and Executives* ■ www.somaticbusinesscoach.com

Matthieu Ricard ■ www.matthieuricard.com ■ www.karuna-shechen.com

Phil Jackson, *Sacred Hoops – Spiritual Lessons of a Hardwood Warrior*, New York: Hyperion Books, 1995

Marianne Williamson, *A Return to Love – Reflections on the Principles of A Course in Miracles* ■ www.marianne.com

Richard Strozzi Heckler, *The Anatomy of Change* ■ www.strozziinstitute.com

John Scherer, *Five Questions that Change Everything* ■ www.the5questions.com ■ www.scherercenter.com

Michael Neill, *Feel Happy Now* ▪ www.geniuscatalyst.com

Laura West, *Center for Joyful Business* ▪ www.JoyfulBusiness.com

Louise L. Hay, *You Can Heal Your Life* ▪ www.hayhouse.com ▪ www.louisehay.com

mary anne radmacher, *Live With Intention*, Conari Press 2010 ▪ www.maryanneradmacher.com

Rosamund Stone Zander and Benjamin Zander, *The Art of Possibility* ▪ www.benjaminzander.com

Thomas G. Crane, *The Heart of Coaching* ▪ www.craneconsulting.com

Brian Tracy ▪ www.briantracy.com

T. Harv Eker, author of #1 NY times Bestseller, *Secrets of the Millionaire Mind* ▪ www.harveker.com

Dewitt Jones ▪ www.dewittjones.com

John Di Lemme ▪ www.ChampionsLiveFree.com

Chris Widener ▪ www.chriswidener.com

Deepak Chopra ▪ www.deepakchopra.com

Melody Beattie ▪ www.melodybeattie.com

Denis Waitley ▪ www.deniswaitley.com

Gary Zukav, *Seat of the Soul* (N.Y.: Simon & Schuster, Inc., 1989 ▪ www.garyzukav.com

Carollyne Conlinn, *Essential Impact* ▪ www.essentialimpact.com

Thomas Leonard ■ www.bestofthomas.com

Andrea J. Lee ■ www.andreajlee.com

Lesley-Ann Marriott ■ www.marriottmanagement.ca

Perdita Felicien ■ www.perditafelicien.blogspot.com / Athletics Canada ■ ■ www.athletics.ca

Michael Phelps ■ www.michaelphelps.com

Lions Gate Chorus, Vancouver, B.C., Canada ■ www.lionsgatechorus.ca

Fandango Quartet ■ www.fandangoquartet.com

me&lewis ideas inc., Vancouver, B.C. ■ www.meehanlewis.com

Deb Carfrae, DLC Designs, North Vancouver, B.C. ■ www.dlcdesigns.net

ABOUT THE AUTHOR
Jan Carley

A certified executive coach, credentialed with the International Coach Federation, Jan brings over 25 years of experience in the professional performing arts to her coaching approach. Her creative thinking and sense of humor, combined with her drive and organizational ability, provide a winning combination for inspiring success and leveraging lasting change.

Jan is committed to facilitating and supporting positive changes in people's lives by "coaching from the inside out." Her company, Creative Coaching Group, specializes in working with highly motivated individuals and high-achieving teams to focus and clarify their energies to achieve a leading edge of excellence. Jan believes that coaching should be a fun and laughter-filled experience and that growth and learning at any stage of life is exciting and liberating.

Known also as the "Inner Coach of Barbershop," Jan is passionate about working with musical groups from the "inside out" to create a more grounded and joyful performance experience both on and off stage. She has been singing barbershop harmony and competing in an Internationally renowned 120-voiced a cappella chorus since 1994.

Jan lives in Vancouver, B.C., Canada, and is available for individual coaching, group coaching, workshops and speaking engagements worldwide.

Contact her at email: jan@creativecoachinggroup.com

www.creativecoachinggroup.com
www.innercoachofbarbershop.com

QUICK ORDER FORM
Harmony From the Inside Out

Online Orders: www.harmonyfromtheinsideout.com

Email inquiries, bulk orders: admin@creativecoachinggroup.com

Telephone Orders: Call 1-604–873-1763

Postal Orders: Please fill out the order form below and mail with a check or money order payment to:
Creative Coaching Group,
775 Sawyer's Lane,
Vancouver, B.C. V5Z 3Z8
CANADA

Name _____

Address _____

City _____ Province or State _____

Postal Code or Zip Code _____

Country_____ Telephone _____

Email Address: * _____

BOOK ORDER

\# of books _____ @ $15.95   = _____

Add Sales Tax: Canadian Residents: Please add 5% GST = _____

Shipping per book: Canada: $5.25 X _____ # books   = _____

USA: $8.25 X _____ # books   = _____

TOTAL ENCLOSED = _____

* You will automatically be subscribed to Creative Coaching Group's email list to receive our monthly online ezine, *Light on the Subject*. You may unsubscribe at any time.